T0321899

Maximizing Information System Availability Through Bayesian Belief Network Approaches:

Emerging Research and Opportunities

Semir Ibrahimović
Bosna Bank International, Bosnia and Herzegovina

Lejla Turulja
University of Sarajevo, Bosnia and Herzegovina

Nijaz Bajgorić
University of Sarajevo, Bosnia and Herzegovina

A volume in the Advances in Business Information Systems and Analytics (ABISA) Book Series

www.igi-global.com

Published in the United States of America by
    IGI Global
    Information Science Reference (an imprint of IGI Global)
    701 E. Chocolate Avenue
    Hershey PA 17033
    Tel: 717-533-8845
    Fax: 717-533-8661
    E-mail: cust@igi-global.com
    Web site: http://www.igi-global.com

                    Library of Congress Cataloging-in-Publication Data

Names: Ibrahimovic, Semir, 1969- author. | Turulja, Lejla, 1981- author. |
   Bajgoric, Nijaz, author.
Title: Maximizing information system availability through bayesian belief
   network approaches : emerging research and opportunities / by Semir
   Ibrahimovic, Lejla Turulja, and Nijaz Bajgoric.
Description: Hershey, PA : Information Science Reference, 2017. | Includes
   bibliographical references.
Identifiers: LCCN 2016057754| ISBN 9781522522683 (hardcover) | ISBN
   9781522522690 (ebook)
Subjects: LCSH: Fault-tolerant computing--Mathematics. | Information storage
   and retrieval systems--Reliability | Financial institutions--Computer
   networks--Reliability. | Bayesian statistical decision theory. | Systems
   availability--Mathematical models.
Classification: LCC QA76.9.F38 I27 2017 | DDC 004.2--dc23 LC record available at https://lccn.
loc.gov/2016057754

This book is published in the IGI Global book series Advances in Business Information Systems
and Analytics (ABISA) (ISSN: 2327-3275; eISSN: 2327-3283)

British Cataloguing in Publication Data
A Cataloguing in Publication record for this book is available from the British Library.

Advances in Business Information Systems and Analytics (ABISA) Book Series

ISSN:2327-3275
EISSN:2327-3283

Editor-in-Chief: Madjid Tavana, La Salle University, USA

MISSION

The successful development and management of information systems and business analytics is crucial to the success of an organization. New technological developments and methods for data analysis have allowed organizations to not only improve their processes and allow for greater productivity, but have also provided businesses with a venue through which to cut costs, plan for the future, and maintain competitive advantage in the information age.

The **Advances in Business Information Systems and Analytics (ABISA) Book Series** aims to present diverse and timely research in the development, deployment, and management of business information systems and business analytics for continued organizational development and improved business value.

COVERAGE

- Data Management
- Data Strategy
- Algorithms
- Performance Metrics
- Business Systems Engineering
- Decision Support Systems
- Big Data
- Information Logistics
- Business Intelligence
- Business Decision Making

IGI Global is currently accepting manuscripts for publication within this series. To submit a proposal for a volume in this series, please contact our Acquisition Editors at Acquisitions@igi-global.com or visit: http://www.igi-global.com/publish/.

Titles in this Series

For a list of additional titles in this series, please visit:
http://www.igi-global.com/book-series/advances-business-information-systems-analytics/37155

Strategic Information Systems and Technologies in Modern Organizations
Caroline Howard (HC Consulting, USA) and Kathleen Hargiss (Colorado Technical University, USA)
Information Science Reference • ©2017 • 366pp • H/C (ISBN: 9781522516804) • US $205.00

Business Analytics and Cyber Security Management in Organizations
Rajagopal (EGADE Business School, Tecnologico de Monterrey, Mexico City, Mexico & Boston University, USA) and Ramesh Behl (International Management Institute, Bhubaneswar, India)
Business Science Reference • ©2017 • 346pp • H/C (ISBN: 9781522509028) • US $215.00

Handbook of Research on Intelligent Techniques and Modeling Applications...
Anil Kumar (BML Munjal University, India) Manoj Kumar Dash (ABV-Indian Institute of Information Technology and Management, India) Shrawan Kumar Trivedi (BML Munjal University, India) and Tapan Kumar Panda (BML Munjal University, India)
Business Science Reference • ©2017 • 428pp • H/C (ISBN: 9781522509974) • US $275.00

Applied Big Data Analytics in Operations Management
Manish Kumar (Indian Institute of Information Technology, Allahabad, India)
Business Science Reference • ©2017 • 251pp • H/C (ISBN: 9781522508861) • US $160.00

Eye-Tracking Technology Applications in Educational Research
Christopher Was (Kent State University, USA) Frank Sansosti (Kent State University, USA) and Bradley Morris (Kent State University, USA)
Information Science Reference • ©2017 • 370pp • H/C (ISBN: 9781522510055) • US $205.00

Strategic IT Governance and Alignment in Business Settings
Steven De Haes (Antwerp Management School, University of Antwerp, Belgium) and Wim Van Grembergen (Antwerp Management School, University of Antwerp, Belgium)
Business Science Reference • ©2017 • 298pp • H/C (ISBN: 9781522508618) • US $195.00

For an enitre list of titles in this series, please visit:
http://www.igi-global.com/book-series/advances-business-information-systems-analytics/37155

www.igi-global.com

701 East Chocolate Avenue, Hershey, PA 17033, USA
Tel: 717-533-8845 x100 • Fax: 717-533-8661
E-Mail: cust@igi-global.com • www.igi-global.com

Table of Contents

Preface

In the e-business economy, most business activities are associated with the use of information technology (IT). Information technology enables and facilitates business, but at the other hand, business success is becoming more dependent on its adequate use and risks associated with that dependence. One of the most important requirements for information systems (IS) is its availability. Availability is the most elementary aspect of assuring value for customers. It assures the customer that services will be available for use under agreed terms and conditions. Availability in the broader sense implies that information system is available to end-users even in the unforeseen and catastrophic events and, at the same time, is protected from various security threats. In other words, at the time the ubiquitous use of information technology, it is expected that information systems are available to provide services to end-users, regardless of time and location.

For this reason, a growing demand for IT services to meet the customers' requirements and expectations is obvious. Service availability has become one of the most important aspects of service delivery in the highly competitive e-business economy. Moreover, service availability has a significant impact on customer satisfaction and the company's reputation. Therefore, great attention is given to several improvements that could provide higher levels of availability of information systems, and therefore higher service availability. However, there are different kinds of risks that may cause the unavailability of information systems, such as human errors, hardware failures, software failures, as well as various disasters. System unavailability can be planned and unplanned. Regular maintenance operations such as upgrades and replacement of software, hardware, communications equipment, and equipment for data storage, data center relocation, may cause system unavailability depending on the system architecture, and in this case we're talking about the planned system unavailability. These activities are planned for a time when their impact on business is minimal, usually late at night on weekends. However, unplanned unavailability is much more problematic because the IT systems failures may result in decreased customer satisfaction, bad publicity, decreased stock prices, lack in fulfillment of regulatory obligations, and decreased reputation of the organization.

The issue of information system availability is especially important for organizations where information systems support real-time business-critical operations, particularly, in the industries in which these systems must continuously operate 24 hours a day, seven days a week, and 365 days a year. Examples of such organizations are process industries, telecommunications, healthcare sector, energy, banking, electronic commerce and more recently, in a variety of cloud services. The financial sector is particularly complex because of the introduction of new channels for selling banking services such as: ATM, POS devices, SMS and Internet that set new demands on availability. Bank's information system should be available 24/7/365 because clients located in any part of the world can have a need for a credit card payment or money transfer using e-banking in any time. Unavailability of financial systems can have major consequences for banks' clients as well as for banks. There are many cases where financial institutions, due to the unavailability of their information system, suffered significant financial losses.

Availability in complex information systems is not measured only for one component, even for one server, but with measuring the availability of services as a whole. In order to achieve higher levels of service availability, it is necessary to ensure the availability of a complex combination of multiple servers (hardware and software) as well as communications and security systems on which this service depends.

Several types of resources are needed in order to achieve a satisfactory system availability. The question is not whether to invest in availability, or not, but how much and in what to invest. The problem is further complicated because it is not easy to carry out cost-benefit analysis for the investment in availability due to the stochastic character of risks. In order to estimate the financial benefits, it is necessary to predict the potential damage that may result from the failure of IT systems. Various mathematical models based on historical data can be used to predict potential losses incurred as a result of operational risks.

In this regard, the main objective of this book is to assist managers in becoming aware of system availability and IT managers in becoming more knowledgeable on the techniques for system availability measuring. This book is intended for scholars as well, academic-oriented objectives of this book are as follows:

- To provide a foundation and a literature review on information system availability and other related concepts, as well as methods for measuring and modeling information system availability.
- To investigate the factors that affect information system availability.
- To provide a model based on the probability that can help with optimization of investments in information security and information system availability in financial institutions.

This book is different from others dealing with the same topic because, besides providing an understanding of the system availability theoretical foundation, it offers the model of information system availability in financial institutions based on Bayesian Belief Network (BBN) approach. . In other words, the book systematically deals with the topic of information system availability in banks and financial institutions, both from the theoretical and practical point of view. All this has a clear practical application and can help managers and IT managers in making decisions on IT-investments in IS-availability. However, bearing in mind the offered model, the book also offers some contributions to the theory of information system availability.

The methodological approach that is used in this book is based on the design of new artifact. Application of *design-science* research in the field of information systems has become very popular recently. The process of artifacts creation relies on existing behavioral theories. IS research can make a significant contribution by conducting complementary research cycle, combining design-science and behavioral science approach to solve the fundamental problems faced by organizations in the application of information technologies. March & Smith (1995) identified two processes (building and evaluation) and four artifacts (constructs, models, methods and instantiations) that are part of the design-science research in IS. The artifacts are made in order to solve previously unsolved problems and evaluated with regard to the contribution they made to solve these problems. It is important to note the difference between working on the system as part of organizations' daily activities and IS research using design-science methodology. The scientific approach includes evaluation, validation, and estimation of the contribution. Formalism, which is base for scientific approach, helps researchers to develop a presentation of IS problem, solutions to problems, as well as the processes of problem solving, which clearly distinguish the knowledge that arise as a product of research.

The book includes six chapters and a conclusion:

- **Chapter One:** The book is structured in a way that the basics of the concept of system availability are presented at the very beginning. In addition to the clarification of the availability concept, determinants and measures, as well as foundation of system availability management are presented in this chapter. Other concepts that are closely related to system availability, i.e. dependability, reliability and maintainability are identified and their brief clarifications are given. Methods and techniques of system availability modeling are presented in this chapter. The three analytical methods for modeling of reliability and availability, as well as alternatives and complements to modeling using BBN such as reliability block diagrams, fault trees and Markov chains are explained. Throughout the chapter, readers have the opportunity to learn what is meant by system availability, how to manage system availability, what the determinants of availability are, and what methods for system availability modeling exist.

- **Chapter Two:** Having laid the foundations of understanding of the availability concept, the following section provides a brief overview of relevant standards for IT security, precisely, system availability. This chapter is divided into two parts. Taking into account that the book will emphasis the importance of system availability in banks and financial institutions, several standards that are relevant for financial institutions such as Basel II and the Payment Card Industry Data Security Standard are presented in the first part of this chapter. All banks and other financial institutions dealing with the payment card transactions are expected to meet the requirements of these two standards. The second part of this chapter provides a short list of most widely used standards for IS security management. From the standpoint of risk management, it is necessary to observe the management of IT operations as a whole, and information security management is only part of that. For this reason, the standards that consider IT function as a whole, ITIL and COBIT, together with ISO 27001: 2013 are described in this section.

- **Chapter Three:** As the spending on IT increase, the awareness on the IT returns is becoming more important. Because of this fact and bearing in mind the importance of system availability, the economic viability of investments in information system availability is presented in this chapter. Since organizations are concerned on how their money invested in IT can be returned, different models and approaches for optimization of investment in system availability are presented. In other words, models that can be used to find an alternative with the most effective or highest achievable outcome in IS availability is one of the main topics of this chapter. The models presented are as follows: return on investment, return on security investment, cost/benefit analysis, analytic hierarchy process, game theory, real options analysis and value at risk security.

- **Chapter Four:** The concept of Bayesian Belief Networks (BBN) is described, as well as building principles and application of BBN and influence diagrams, and the reasons why BBN are considered an adequate tool for IS availability modeling. The main reason for choosing this instrument is its applicability in the treatment of problems of this domain. The Bayesian network is constructed through two phases: i) the relevant variables and (causal) relations among them are identified; and ii) sets of conditional probability distributions are specified. Also in this chapter, we presented utility theory and application of Bayesian methods in decision-making. As tools for BBN application in decision making, we described decision trees and influence diagram. This chapter also contains some directions on when is appropriate to use BBN in decision making process.
- **Chapter Five:** Provides presentation of the method that is used to measure and maximize IS availability. The method of selection of independent variables with a detailed definition of each of the variables in the model is described. This section contains the model based on Bayesian network, utility theory, and influence diagrams. Also in this chapter, we presented model parameterization procedure and gave theoretical background as well, as practical steps for experts' elicitation. Finally, we presented results of running the model by using Genie 2.0 BBN software.
- **Chapter Six:** Described implementation of proposed model by using Monte-Carlo simulation. In the first part of this chapter the influence diagram has been validated using the Monte-Carlo analysis in which each variable takes values from the distribution emerged from the elicitation, instead of using average values as in the influence diagram. In the second part of this chapter, we used the Crystal ball optimization tool for solving the model. In an attempt to find the optimal solution that maximizes the average value of the utility function, we made an analysis with 10,000 "what if" scenarios and, in each scenario, we changed 10,000 different values of the variables. At the end of this section, we discussed the simulation results and compared them with the results we got in solving the influence diagram. In third section of this

chapter we used Monte-Carlo simulation to construct "efficient frontier" function (Markowitz, 1952). This function determines optimal investment level and optimal investment portfolio for given (desired) availability level.

The book's conclusion contains concluding remarks, methodology constraints and directions for a future research.

REFERENCES

Brynjolfsson, E., & Kahin, B. (2000). *Understanding the Digital Economy; Data, Tools, and Research*. Massachusetts Institute of Technology.

March, S. T., & Smith, G. F. (1995). Design and natural science research on information technology. *Decision Support Systems*, *15*(4), 251–266. doi:10.1016/0167-9236(94)00041-2

Markowitz, H. (1952). Portfolio Selection. *The Journal of Finance*, *7*(1), 77–91.

Chapter 1
Information System Availability:
Definition and Business Perspective

ABSTRACT

In order to provide better understanding of the availability concept, it is necessary to define and review the terms that shape a framework for information systems availability. This section introduces the concept of availability and the three terms that are most associated with the concept of availability, namely: dependability, reliability and maintainability. A short introduction to availability modeling is also presented in this section by explaining three most widely used methods; Reliability Block Diagrams, Fault Trees Diagrams, and Markov Chains.

INFORMATION SYSTEM, IT ARCHITECTURES, AND DOWNTIME

In today's world, most business activities are associated with the use of information technology. Information technology enables and facilitates business processes. In addition, business success is becoming more dependent on the adequate use of information technologies, and risks associated with this dependence. Definition of the "Information technology" term is adopted from ITIL glossary where IT refers to "the use of technology for the stor-

DOI: 10.4018/978-1-5225-2268-3.ch001

age, communication or processing of information. The technology typically includes computers, telecommunications, applications and other software".

Modern businesses employ several information technologies such as servers, desktop computers, portable/mobile computing devices, operating systems, application software, data communication (networking) technologies by implementing them in several forms of business (enterprise) information systems. These information systems are in most cases built on client-server model of information architecture model which consists of server(s) and clients (desktop computers and mobile devices) with applications installed on server computers. A client/server-based information architecture divides processing into two major categories: clients and servers. A client is a computer such as a PC or a workstation attached to a computer network consisting of several dozens (hundreds or thousands) clients and one or more servers. Server's side of such an information architecture is called "Business Server", "Enterprise Server" or "Server Operating Environment". It consists of standard server-based and additional continuous computing technologies that are used to enhance key server platform features such as reliability, availability, and scalability. Servers can be installed "on premises" (standard "client-server" model) or in the "cloud" (cloud computing provider' premises, "client-cloud" model). In the digital age, server configurations and server operating systems that run them are expected to provide such an operating environment that must meet rigorous requirements with regard to system uptime and application availability.

As the client-server model of information architecture is most widely used for all enterprise information systems (ERP, SCM, CRM, BI), in both on-premises and cloud-based infrastructures, the server side of such an architecture determines the availability of applications installed on application servers. EIS applications are installed on enterprise servers that are run by server operating systems. Therefore, availability, reliability and scalability of these systems is of extreme importance for modern organizations. Such environment created a particular business pressure of being "up-and-running" for many businesses. Server operating systems (SOS) play crucial role in keeping business "in-business" as their crashes are one of the main reasons of "going out of business."

When it comes to modern e-business applications, system downtime is simply not an option. Several industries such as banks, financial institutions, airline reservation systems, point-of-sale systems, dispatching systems, online shops must be running on "always-on" basis.

Today's enterprises are exposed to several types of threats coming from outside and inside the system such as:

AVAILABILITY AND RELATED TERMS

In order to provide better understanding of the availability concept, it is necessary to review and define the terms that shape a framework for information systems availability. Three terms that are most associated with the concept of availability are: dependability, reliability and maintainability. These terms will first be explained as an introduction to the availability concept.

Dependability

Dependability is a broader concept of availability and it is defined as "property of a computer system such that reliance can justifiably be placed on the service it delivers" (Laprie & Roche, 1995). The service delivered by a system is its behavior as it is perceptible by its users who interact with the system. User of the system can be human or another system. Dependability describes the ability of a system to deliver service in a way such that non-functional demands are fulfilled (Troger, Feinbube, & Werner, 2016).

The concept of dependability is especially researched and applied in the areas of real-time systems and systems with high safety standards (nuclear technology) (Verma, Ajit, & Kumar, 2011; Matthiesen, Hamouda, Kaaniche, & Schwefel, 2008; Courtois, 2008; Tambe, Balasubramanian, Gokhale, & Damiano, 2007). Since information systems in financial institutions must respond to users' requests in real time, paradigm of dependability can be applied to such systems as well. Depending on the area where this concept is applied, different aspects of the paradigm are emphasized. The main focus of this book is on the information system availability and relating concepts.

Avižienis, Laprie, & Randell (2001) proposed a systematic exposition of the concepts of dependability that consists of three parts: the threats to, the attributes of, and the means by which dependability is attained, as shown in Figure 2.

Figure 2. The fundamental chain of dependability and security threats
Source: Avizienis, Laprie, Randell, & Landwehr, 2004

The Threats

The threats to dependability are faults, errors and failures that are undesired circumstances resulting from un-dependability (Laprie & Roche, 1995). Faults are defined as a "defect in the hardware component or device; for example, a short circuit or broken wire, an incorrect step, process or data definition in a computer program"(IEEE, 1990). The error is that the part of the system that may cause a subsequent failure: failure occurs when the error reaches the service interface and alerts the service (Avižienis et al., 2001). On the other side, a fault is the adjudged or hypothesized cause of an error. The fault can cause a system error whereupon becomes active; otherwise, it sleeps, i.e. it is dormant.

The error is "difference between a computed, observed, or measured value or condition and the true, specified, or theoretically correct value or condition" (IEEE, 1990). For example, deviation in the specified time for a financial transaction is the error. Errors can be detected; in which case it produces messages or signals of an error. If the error in the system propagates the edge of the system and lead to the inability to deliver contracted services within the agreed specifications, then it is the system failure. The flow from the fault through error to failure is shown in the Figure 2.

The Attributes

Various classifications of dependability attributes are present in the literature. For example, Verma, Ajit, & Kumar (2011) suggest reliability, availability and reversibility as dependability attributes. On the other side, Avizienis et al. (2004) suggested more attributes of dependability such as:

- **Availability:** Readiness to provide correct service.
- **Reliability:** Continuity of correct services.
- **Safety:** The absence of catastrophic consequences on the users and/or the environment.
- **Confidentiality:** Absence of unauthorized access to information.
- **Integrity:** Lack of correct information changes.
- **Maintainability:** Modifications and repairs ability.

The Means

The third component of dependability are the means for managing defects and according to Avizienis et al., (2004) they include:

- **Fault Prevention:** Means to prevent the occurrence or introduction of faults.
- **Fault Tolerance:** Means to avoid service failures in the presence of faults.
- **Fault Removal:** Means to reduce the number and severity of faults.
- **Fault Forecasting:** Means to estimate the present number, the future incidence, and the likely consequences of faults.

The main goal of the error prevention and fault tolerance is to provide the ability to deliver a service that can be trusted. Fault removal and fault forecasting seek to achieve the goal of confidence in that ability by justifying that the functional and the dependability & security specifications are adequate and that the system is likely to meet them (Laprie et al., 2004).

Reliability

According to the IEEE definition, reliability is "the ability of a system or component to perform its required functions under stated conditions for a specified period of time" (IEEE, 1990). Thus, for any time interval $(z, z + t]$ reliability $R\ (t \mid z)$ is the probability that the system does not fail within a specified period of time, assuming that it is working at time z (Grottke, Sun, Fricks, & Trivedi, 2008). Reliability is measured using the following parameters: the ratio between the number of reliable responses and total number of requests - Reliable response ratio (RRR); the number of wrong answers in the specified period of time - Service Failure Ratio (SFR); and the average time between two wrong answers - Mean Time Between Failure Service (MTBFS) (Bayram, Kirlidog, & Vayvay, 2010).

RRR is calculated as:

$$RRR = \frac{\text{the number of reliable responses}}{\text{total number of requests}} \tag{1}$$

RRR is calculated as:

$$SFR = \frac{\text{the number of wrong answers}}{\text{period of time}} \tag{2}$$

Mean time between two false responses can be calculated as the sum of the time intervals in which the system was operational divided by the number of incidents:

$$\text{MTBFS} = \frac{\sum\left(\text{start of downtime} - \text{start of uptime}\right)}{\text{number of failures}} \tag{3}$$

Above formulas reflect that the metric of reliability is not affected by the length of service interruption, but only by the number of incorrect responses to the service requests in the observed time period.

Maintainability

Maintainability is the system ability which measures "the ease with which a software system or component can be modified to correct faults, improve performance or other attributes, or adapt to a changed environment" (IEEE, 1990). ITIL defines this term as a measure which measures the rate of system return and/or service after the failure to normal operation. This size is usually expressed as a mean of time required for recovery service - mean time to restore (MTRS). Mean time to restore is different from the mean time to repair (MTTR), with which it is often confused, because the time it takes to fix bugs and add the time it takes to restore service TRS = TTR + TimeToRecover (Taylor, Iqbal, et al., 2007). MTRS depends on several factors including: configuration of service assets; mean time to repair (MTTR) of individual components; competency of support staff; resources available including information; policies, procedures, and guidelines; redundancy, etc. Corrections of these factors individually, or in combination, increase maintainability. Figure 3 presents improvement opportunities within incident lifecycle, i.e. reducing any of the factors (time to record, time to respond, time to resolve, time to repair) can reduce MTRS.

Availability

IEEE defines availability as "the degree to which a system or component is operational and accessible when required for use. Often expressed as a probability" (IEEE, 1990). It means that availability is a measure of the readiness of the system to be used when required for the purpose it was designed for. Carnegie Mellon Institute, within the framework of the model of maturity service, gives a more complex definition: "Availability is the degree to which

Figure 3. Improvement opportunities within incident lifecycle
Source: Taylor, Iqbal, & Nieves (2007)

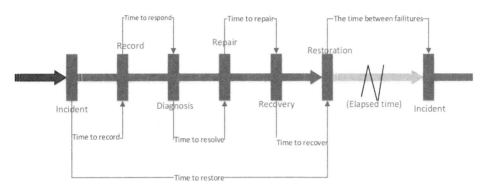

something is accessible and usable when needed". In the context of services, "availability can refer to the set of times, places, and other circumstances in which services are to be delivered, service requests are to be honored, or other aspects of a service agreement are to be valid" (CMMI, 2010). CMMI considers availability as a quality attribute. It is possible to have different definitions and measurements of availability for different types of services and systems and for the different perspectives of availability, for example: business perspective, the perspective of the end user, the customer's perspective, the perspective of the service provider etc. (CMMI, 2010).

ISO 27000 series of standards applied availability to the concept of organizational assets. The asset is available if it is accessible and ready for use at the request of an authorized entity. In the context of this standard, the assets include things such as information, systems, facilities, networks and computers (ISO/IEC, 2012). Singh (2009) gives a more quantitative definition where for the observed system S, Ps Availability of S system is the probability that the system is operational and ready to provide services. Since the Ps is a number that should be close to 100% as much as it is possible, common way to represent the system availability is to count the nines. So, 99.999% availability is called as "five nines". The following table shows the relationship between the number of nines and time of system unavailability.

Availability is also defined as a combination of three concepts: reliability, accessibility and timeliness (Somasundaram & Shrivastava, 2009). When explaining information availability, Somasundaram & Shrivastava (2009) considered reliability as "component's ability to function without failure, under stated conditions, for a specified amount of time"; accessibility as "the state within which the required information is accessible at the right place, to the right user" and timeliness as "exact moment or the time window dur-

Table 1. The ratio of the number of nines and system availability

Number of Nines	Availability	Annual Time of Unavailability in Minutes	Practical Meaning
1	90%	52596.00	Unavailable for 5 weeks per year
2	99%	5259.60	Unavailable for 4 weeks per year
3	99.9%	525.96	Unavailable for 9 hours per year
4	99.99%	52.60	Unavailable for 1 hour per year
5	99.999%	5.26	Unavailable for 5 minutes per year
6	99.9999%	0.53	Unavailable for 30 seconds per year
7	99.99999%	0.05	Unavailable for 3 seconds per year

ing which information must be accessible". System can be in an accessible or inaccessible state. The period of time during which the system is in an accessible state is termed "system uptime". At the other hand, "system downtime" is period when it is not accessible.

Harper, Lawler, & Thornton (2005) introduced the concept of disaster tolerance and emphasized its importance. Unlike the term disaster recovery that represents the ability to continue operations after a disaster, disaster tolerance is the ability of the organization to continue operations without interruption despite the occurrence of catastrophic events.

Availability is often referred to as the part of CIA triangle of information security - Confidentiality, Integrity, Availability (Ioannidis, Pym, & Williams, 2009; Martin & Khazanchi, 2006; Bodin, Gordon, & Loeb, 2004; Bodin, Gordon, & Loeb, 2008; Faisst & Prokein, 2006). In addition, there is an approach that considers availability together with information system resilience where this term refers to a system's capability to "provide and maintain an acceptable level of service in the face of various faults and challenges to normal operation" (Liu, Deters, & Yhang, 2009), which is very close to the original definition of availability. This term is also used by (Bajgoric, 2008) as a synonym for business continuity. Business resilience can be seen as the ability of business organizations to quickly adapt and respond to internal or external dynamic changes and/or opportunities, demands, disruptions or threats, and continue operations with limited impact on the functionality. In this sense, the concept of resistance can be considered through six layers: strategy, organization, processes, data and applications, technologies and facilities. Schiesser (2010) considered availability as the process of optimizing the readiness of production systems for accurate measurement, analysis and reduction of these systems' disruption. He distinguishes availability and system uptime, noting that the availability is a characteristic of the system visible to the customer, while the continuous operation of the system should be considered in relation to suppliers. Somasundaram & Shrivastava (2009) considered the concept of business continuity as an integrated overall process at the organizational level, which includes all activities (IT and others) that the organization must take to mitigate the impact of planned and unplanned interruptions in the availability of the system.

Measuring Availability

In general, availability is measured as the ratio of time in which the system was available in comparison to the total time of use.

The basic formula for measuring the availability of the system is:

$$Availability = \frac{System\,uptime}{System\,uptime + System\,downtime} \tag{4}$$

System uptime of complex systems is the sum of the required uptime of all subsystem. For example, if it is observed a system that provides the following services with the agreed times of availability: core banking 24*7, SWIFT 8*5, e-banking 24*7, m-banking 24*7, then the required system uptime is 52*(24*7*8+5+7+24*24*7) = 28,288 hours per year. For the system downtime, each service downtime should be summed up taking into account the percentage of affected users.

Apart from previous formula, some authors suggested the following one as well:

$$Availability = \frac{MTTF}{MTTF + MTTR} \tag{5}$$

where MTTR (Mean Time to Repair) corresponds to the mean time to repair the faults of the system, including the time of detection of failure, repair time, and period of system return to the operating state. This practically means that once the failure has occurred, the system will require MTTR hours on the average for recovery. MTTF (Mean Time to Failure) represents the mean time between failures. The formula shows that the availability of the system does not depend on the distribution of faults, but only of the mean time between failures and the time required for system repair. In this model, the implicit assumption is that repairs can always be performed in a manner to restore system to its original, best condition, i.e. to be as good as new (Grottke et al., 2008).

However, other ways of measurement can be found in the literature. Therefore, in order to establish appropriate measurement of system redundancy, and therefore availability, Bauer, Adams, & Eustace (2011) highlighted the key outage measurement concepts: formal definition of total and partial outage, normalization units, minimum chargeable service disruption duration, outage attributability, system and network elements attributes, and treatment of planned events.

Carnegie Mellon Institute proposed a broader approach to measuring the availability by proposing the following measures:

- Percentage available within agreed hours (this availability can be overall service availability or service component availability);
- Percentage unavailable within agreed hours (this unavailability can be overall service unavailability or service component unavailability);
- Duration of downtime due to failure (typically minutes, hours, or hours per week) Failure frequency;
- Scope of impact (e.g., number of users who were affected, number of minutes that users lost productivity, number of transactions or vital business functions not processed or carried out, number of application services impeded);
- Response time of the service system to service incidents, transaction response times, and service response times (this response time can be a capacity measure or availability measure); and
- Reliability (e.g., number of service breaks, mean time between failures, mean time between) (CMMI, 2010).

Availability Determinants

Different classifications of availability determinants are present in the literature, and it depends on the research approach and authors which classification will be used. Most common determinants in literature are listed below.

Martin & Khazanchi (2006) identified seven key determinants of availability: physical security, auditing and system effectiveness evaluation, security policy, redundancy, system monitoring and operational control, business continuity and backups. Franke, Johnson, König, & Marcks von Würtemberg (2012) proposed model with 16 determinants that affect the availability based on the "availability index" which was introduced by Marcus & Stern

(2003): Physical environment, requirements and procurement, operations, change control, technical solution of backup, process solution of backup, data redundancy, storage architecture redundancy, structure redundancy, avoidance of internal application failures, avoidance of external services that fail, network redundancy, avoidance of network failures, physical location, resilient client/server solutions, and monitoring of the relevant components. Furthermore, Bajgoric (2008) identified eight the IT-related threats that may cause system unavailability: physical threats, natural threats, logical threats, technical glitches and/or hardware components failures, application software defects, failures and crashes, WAN/Internet-specific infrastructure problems, human errors, and loss of key IT personal or leaving of expert staff. Ibrahimovic & Bajgoric (2015) suggested a model of 13 determinants which draws on Franke et al.'s model. EMC conducted an extensive study on 250 European companies from different industries and of different sizes in 2011 in order to understand the real causes of business interruption and to measure the economic impacts from IT downtime. The found three most common causes of data loss and downtime to be:

- **Hardware Failure:** 61 percent.
- **Power Failure:** 42 percent.
- **Data Corruption:** 35 percent.

Managing Availability

System's manageability refers to the capability of a system to be managed and how easy the interaction with the system can be conducted. According to Liu, Deters, & Yhang (2009) manageability of a system depends on the manageability of its subsystems and components.

Based on the above formulas, there are two ways to improve the availability: increasing the time between failures (TTF) and reducing the time required for recovery (TTR). In order to increase the TTF, firms should apply proactive techniques aiming to avoid failures. For example, firms can prevent failures associated with software "aging" using the techniques of "rejuvenation". To reduce TTR, Trivedi et al. (2008) proposed escalated levels of recovery, so that most failures were fixed by the quickest recovery method and only few by the slowest ones.

Various recommendations for enhancing both availability and system's manageability can be found in literature. Some of them are listed here: an enterprise architecture analysis approach (Liu et al., 2009; Raderius, Narman, & Ekstedt, 2009), improving security policies (Martin & Khazanci, 2006), virtualization (Gay, 2007), clustering and virtualization (Calzolari, 2006), the application of standards in the IS management (Bajgoric, Spremic, & Turulja, 2011), contingency planning approach (R. Harris & Grimalla, 2008). Chen, Kataria, & Krishnan (2011) suggested a strategy of diversification as a possible solution to reduce the unavailability of the system in case that the unavailability was caused by attacks on network resources. Clark (2010) proposed approach to increase the system availability with creation of a contingency plan that can protect an organization from going out-of-business. The greater amount of information means that an organization may be more vulnerable now then anytime in the past to natural disasters that may destroy an organization and its numerous customer records (Clark, 2010). That is the reason why organizations should invest in different approaches in order to protect themselves and their clients. Clark (2010) suggested that all organization should prepare themselves for disaster events with contingency planning consisting of four basic aspects: business impact analysis, incident response plan, disaster recovery plan, and business continuity plan. He also emphasized the importance of regular testing of these plans. In order to improve the availability, Bell (2005) proposed the use of best practices when designing a data center. Furthermore, the importance of technology clustering and servers mirroring for system availability are recognized as important practices. This concept implies that two servers that are situated on the same or different physical locations work in pairs, with the same information. If one server fails, the other takes over complete load.

Cai (2008) addressed the problem of the availability management in large enterprise applications and systems in terms of the relationship between performance and availability. He proposed an approach to business policy-driven, risk-based, automated availability management, which used an automated decision engine to make availability decisions and meet business policies while optimizing overall system utility. He used utility theory to capture users' risk attitudes, and addressed the potentially conflicting business goals and resource demands in enterprise scale distributed systems (Cai, 2008).

Scott (1999), based on Gartner Group research, concluded that approximately 80 percent of unplanned downtime is caused by people and process issues, while the remainder is caused by technology failures and disasters. He wrote:

Based on extensive feedback from clients, we estimate that, on average, unplanned application downtime is caused... : 20 percent of the time by hardware (e.g., server and network), OSs, environmental factors (e.g., heating, cooling and power failures) and disasters; 4 failures including "bugs," performance issues or changes to 40 percent of the time by application applications that cause problems (including the application code itself or layered software on which the application is dependent); and 40 percent of the time by operator errors, including not performing a required operations task or performing a task incorrectly. (Scott, 1999)

The bottom line conclusion of his work is that organizations should not let infrastructure redundancy provide a false sense of availability assurance. To address the 80 percent of unplanned downtime caused by people and process failures, enterprises should invest in improving IT processes (suggested investment strategies provided at Figure 4) (Scott, 1999).

Furthermore, Gartner's research conducted in 2009 was based on the metric as a prerequisite for managing availability. They recommend ITIL v.3 metric that measures the availability of services to the business, so-called availability between endpoints (end-to-end). These measures are not oriented towards measuring the availability of the components (base, networks or servers) but only the availability of services to the end user. In this sense, determining the metric depends on the end user priorities, and those variables that can affect the availability and performance of services from the perspective of

Figure 4. Causes of Unplanned Downtime
Source: Scott, 1999

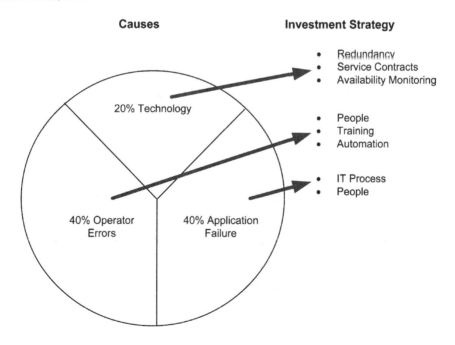

the end user are measured. Consequently, Scott (2009) recommends following actions: measuring of the availability of key services as a mandatory; improvements in the life cycle of software development in the sense that the demands on availability are taken into account in the early stages of software design; planning time for maintenance of individual services instead of a single time in which to maintain all services system.

In addition to reports on the availability, Gartner regularly analyze and make review of the maturity of technology for business continuity and disaster recovery. Figure 5 shows such a review whose aim is to help identifying important processes and technologies, their level of adoption and modifying their management strategies toward a mature BCM (Gartner, 2011).

An important contribution to this subject is also given by Carnegie Mellon Institute that defined the CERT Resilience Management Model (CERT-RMM) which describes the essential processes for managing operations resistance and provides a structure from which an organization can begin with business continuity process improvement, IT security, and other orga-

Figure 5. Hype Cycle for Business Continuity Management and IT Disaster Recovery Management, 2011 expectations
Source: Gartner Report, 2011

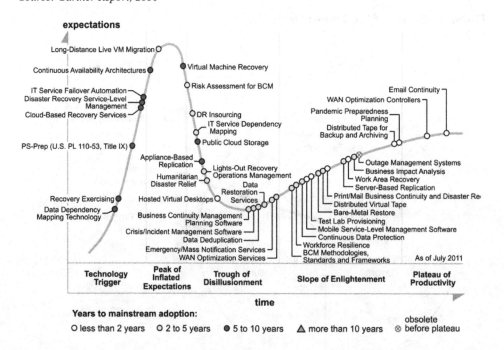

nizational efforts. In addition, CERT-RMM is the first known model that includes the dimension of capability in the domain of security and business continuity. The main characteristics of this model are:

- **Provides a Deep Process Definition Across Four Categories:** Enterprise management, engineering, operations management, and process management;
- **Focuses on Four Essential Operational Assets:** People, information, technology, and facilities;
- **Includes Processes and Practices that Define Four Capability Levels for Each Process Area:** Incomplete, Performed, Managed, and Defined;
- Serves as a meta-model that includes references to common codes of practice such as ISO27000, ITIL, COBIT, and others such as BS25999 and ISO24762;
- Includes process metrics and measurements that can be used to ensure that operational resilience processes are performing as intended; and
- Facilitates an objective measurement of capability levels via a structured and repeatable appraisal method (SunGard White Paper Series, 2012).

IBM has also carried out numerous studies analyzing the system availability. They introduced the concept of bounded systems in 1999. Bounded system is a system that aims to achieve high availability and it includes the following technologies and processes: application management, availability management, capacity management, change management, metric management, network management, problem management, performance management, service level management and system recovery management (IBM Global Services Report, 1999). Afterwards, in 2007, they used the term business resilience, in order to emphasize a broader approach that involves a comprehensive strategy in contrast to terms that present narrower approaches such as disaster recovery, high availability, security and business continuity. Using term from the concept of an object-oriented technology, IBM has created a business resilience framework that is designed to help identifying the object layers that make up company, ranging from the strategies that govern business, all the way down to the nuts-and-bolts technologies and facilities (Cocchiara, 2007). Based on the cross industrial research on key drivers of business resistance implementation conducted on a sample of 391 companies of various sizes from different parts of the world 2011, IBM has identified the most successful techniques for raising the level of business resistance:

data and application, data protection, infrastructure security, security governance, identity and access management and compliance management (as shown in Figure 6).

AVAILABILITY MODELING

A brief literature overview on the reliability and availability modeling will be given in this section. Raderius et al. (2009) suggested two most frequently used modeling techniques: reliability block diagrams and Monte-Carlo simulation. According to them, the lack of these methods is inability to express uncertainty as well as model high dependency of the architecture of the system being modeled. In general, methods of availability modeling can be divided into three broader categories: analytical, quantitative and qualitative (Malek, Milic, & Milanovic, 2008; Trivedi et al., 2008).

Quantitative models are based on measurements and are most often used on the system hardware components, while difficult to apply to services due to insufficient availability of metrics and measurement instruments. Qualitative models are conducted less formally. The main tools used for qualitative modeling are questionnaires and interviews. Qualitative models are susceptible to misinterpretation because mutual comparison is hardly feasible. These

Figure 6. IT components of enterprise management (percent of all respondents)
Source: IBM Report, 2011

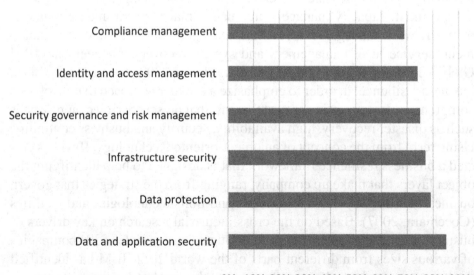

models are very dependent on the knowledge of the consultant who carried out modeling as well. Trivardi et al. (2008) describe qualitative models as models based on verbal descriptions and checklists, while qualitative models are stochastic models constructed on the basis of hardware and software system architecture. Some of qualitative models are: CMMI, ITIL, CITIL, ISO/IEC 15504 - SPICE, COBIT, MOF, MITO, ISO/IEC 27002 and ISO 12207/IEEE 12207, etc. (Milanovic, 2010).

Analytical methods use mathematical tools for modeling and simulation of services. Analytical methods for modeling the system availability that can be found in literature are: reliability block diagrams, fault trees, reliability graphs and complex configurations, Markov models, stochastic petri nets, stochastic activity networks, Markov reward models etc. In addition to the analysis of methods for system availability modeling, Milanovic (2010) presented an analysis of software tools for modeling availability: Isograph Reliability Workbench, Mobius, SHARPE, OpenSESAME and other. Some of these tools have a specialized application; for example, Network Availability Program (NAP) is intended to assess the availability and reliability in communication networks. NAP analyzes how defects in network elements can affect the flow of data between the source and destination nodes in the network.

Unlike most of the models that model system availability binary (system available or not available), Tokuno & Yamada (2008), in their approach to modeling software intensive systems, identify drop of system performance as a condition that affects the availability. Looking at the system from the end users perspective, they distinguish two states of the system: the state when the system has performance in accordance with the specifications, and the state when performance is below specified. They used Markov processes as a tool for modeling the system availability. This process describes the time-dependent behavior of the system alternating between up and down state (Tokuno & Yamada, 2008). In another research, they modeled the availability of the system in terms of the number of restoration actions using the same tool (Tokuno & Yamada, 2000). They correlated the failure and restoration characteristics of the software system with the cumulative number of corrected faults considering an imperfect debugging environment where the detected faults are not always corrected and removed from the system. Markov processes are used by Goyal & Lavenberg (1987) as well. They made high-level model to describe the failure and repair behavior of the components that comprise a system, including important component interactions, and the repair actions that are taken when components fail. Immonen & Niemelä (2007) defined the framework for the comparison of methods for the analysis of reliability and availability from the software architecture point of view. They gave an overview of the advantages and disadvantages of the methods for predicting the availability and research activities that must be carried out in order to overcome the identified deficiencies. The comparison of the methods revealed that none of the studied methods alone could provide adequate support for predicting reliability and availability from software architecture.

In the sections that follow, three analytical methods for modeling reliability and availability, as well as alternatives and complements to modeling using BBN will be presented: reliability block diagrams, fault trees and Markov chains.

Reliability Block Diagrams

Reliability Block Diagram (RBD) is a modeling tool that is used to study complex systems (Doguc, 2010). In RBD, system components and subsystems are presented with different blocks that are connected in series or in parallel. Using RBD, it is possible to do a budget which assesses the frequency of errors, the mean time between failures (MTBF) as well as reliability and availability of the system. Calculations can be changed by modifying the configuration of RBD and thus create multiple scenarios of system behavior in different configurations.

The reliability block diagram is a diagram of events. Using RBD, the following question can be answered: what are the elements necessary to fulfill the specified system's functions and which elements can be out of service without affecting the functionality of the system? Setting RBD includes, as a first step, partitioning the system into elements with clearly defined tasks. The elements required for the specified system function are connected in series, while the elements which may be out of operation without affecting the function (redundant) are connected in parallel. The order of elements connected in series can be arbitrary. Elements that are not relevant to meet the specified function of the considered system are not included in the diagram (Birolini, 2014). RBD may consist of serial subsystems, parallel subsystems, or their combinations. There is no redundancy in serial subsystems, i.e. if one component fails, the whole subsystem becomes unavailable. On the other hand, in a parallel subsystem with m components, subsystem continues to work even when only one of the components works. This result is achieved by redundant arrangement of tasks of each of the parallel components. Parallel and serial subsystems are used together in many real life situations. Figure 7 shows an example of block diagram system composed of a combination of serial and parallel subsystems.

Figure 7. RBD combination of serial and parallel systems
Source: Doguc (2010)

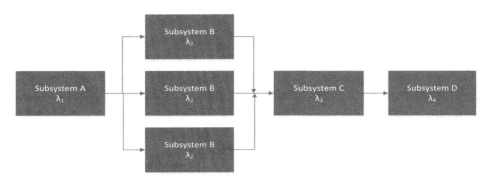

RBD can also be used in Monte Carlo simulations to determine the changes on unreliability, availability, and overall system performance, without any modification of the system itself.

The primary value of RBD is in highlighting the Single Point of Failure (SPOF) in the design. Any non-redundant module on the critical path is, by definition, single point of failure. RBD emphasizes essential modules for the service providing as a first step in the analysis of reliability. This step clearly shows the modules that should be taken into account in the analysis of failures and in architecture-based availability modeling (Bauer, 2010).

Naive interpretation of the block diagram topology of reliability or other architectural diagrams can lead to misperceptions that optimal improvement opportunity (without considering costs) in any high-availability architecture is always the removal of SPOFs. However, the analyst may fail to realize from the diagram that the structure of the system is just one of many factors that determine the importance of the component in high-availability systems. Other decisive factors are, for example: availability/unavailability of the components of the system, the mission time, and target availability. In addition, the adoption of a hierarchical approach in modeling can lead to confusion too. For example, the subsystem that appears as SPOFs in high-level diagrams may correspond to highly redundant components structure (Grottke et al., 2008).

Fault Trees Diagrams

Fault Trees Diagram (FTD) is another tool that is often used to assess the reliability of the system. Similar to RBD, FTD represent all sequences of individual component failures that may cause the system to stop functioning.

Fault trees apply deductive logic to produce a fault-oriented pictorial diagram which allows the analysis of the safety and reliability of the system. The main difference between fault trees diagrams and reliability block diagrams is that with RBS one is working in the success space – looking for the combination of components that allow normal operation of the system (success). In contrast, the fault tree diagram is generated in failure space identifying all possible combinations of failures of components that lead to a system failure (Milanovic, 2010).

The starting point of every fault tree is the definition of a single, well-defined and undesirable event (e.g. system failure), which represents the root of a tree. The tree is then built using top-down approach, combining logic gates (such as AND and OR) and events. Each gate has at least two inputs and one output; outputs of other gates and events can be inputs. The reduction process stops when it reaches the main event for which further reduction is not needed. The probability level of a higher level event can be calculated by combining the probability of lower level events.

In the following section, the basics of the diagram functioning will be explained assuming mutual independence of the main events. In an OR gate, the output event occurs if at least one of the input events occurs. In terms of the reliability of the system, this means that a fail of any component (input) implies a system fail (output). In RBD, the equivalent is a series configuration, as shown in Figure 8.

Reliability and availability of OR gate with n inputs are:

$$R_{OR} = \prod_{I=1}^{n} R_i \tag{6}$$

Figure 8. OR gate - FT diagram with equivalent RBD

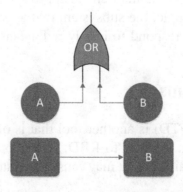

$$A_{OR} = \prod_{I=1}^{n} A_i \tag{7}$$

wherein R_i and A_i are reliability and availability of each component, respectively. At AND gate, output event occurs if all input events occur. In the context of the analysis of the system reliability, this implies that all components must fail (input) in order for the system to fail (output). In RBD terminology, equivalent to the AND gate is a simple parallel configuration. Reliability and availability of the gates with n inputs are:

$$R_{AND} = 1 - \prod_{I=1}^{n} (1 - R_i) \tag{8}$$

$$A_{AND} = 1 - \prod_{I=1}^{n} (1 - A_i) \tag{9}$$

The third basic fault tree gate is a special case of OR gate in which at least k out of n input events (k <n) should occur in order for an output event to occur. In terms of the reliability of the system, this means that if k or more system components fail (input), it will lead to fail of the entire system (output). The formulas for calculating the reliability and availability of this gate are:

$$R_{K|N} = \sum_{i=n-k+1}^{n} \binom{n}{i} R^i (1 - R)^{n-i} \tag{10}$$

$$A_{K|N} = \frac{MTTF_{K|N}}{MTTF_{K|N} + MTTR_{K|N}} \tag{11}$$

The Figure 9 shows an example of fault tree in the computer system: The advantages of FTD use are listed below:

- Enables use of reliable information about the components failures and other basic events to assess the overall risk associated with the design of a new system with lack of historical data.
- Eases understanding and implementation.

Figure 9. Fault tree of the fault-tolerant computer system
Source: Milanovic, 2010

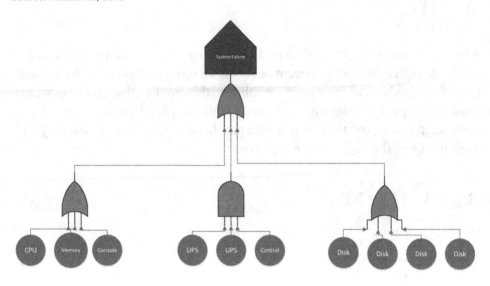

- Offers a qualitative description of potential problems and the combination of events that cause problems.
- Enables quantitative assessment of the probability and frequency of failures and the relative importance of the various sequences of faults and other events that may cause a problem.
- Provides compiling lists of recommended actions for the prevention of problems.
- Provides quantitative evaluation of effectiveness of the recommendations.

Limitations of FTD use are:

- Difficult to imagine all possible scenarios that lead to undesired event?
- Construction of tree for large systems can be tiresome?
- Correlation between the main events (e.g. failure of components belonging to the same series) is difficult to model and accurate solutions for modeling event correlation does not exist.
- Subjective decisions about the level of details and completeness are often needed. (Pandey, 2000)

Markov Chains

Combinatorial methods such as RBD, FTD or reliability graphs are based on the assumption of stochastic independence between components: failure or recovery of system component is not caused by other components. In cases where it is necessary to model the complex interactions between components of the system, other types of models must be used. One example of such system is a system with four nodes which evenly distribute the load (load balancing). If failure of one node occurs, the other three will become more burdened which probably affects the degree of their reliability. Such behavior cannot be modeled with tools that assume independence between system components. Alternative models that can be used for these systems are Markov models.

Markov models are based on stochastic processes. A stochastic process is a family of random variables defined on a sample space. As a random variable describes the statistical random occurrence, so the stochastic process is a set of random variables $X(t)$, one for each time t in a set of J. The set S in which the random variable $X(t)$ assumes a value is names a sample space. The state space can be either discrete or continuous. If the state space is discrete, the process is called a chain. Time as a parameter of stochastic process can also be discrete or continuous (Milanovic, 2010).

Markov methods are useful tools for evaluating the availability of systems with more states (available, unavailable, and partially available). The Figure 10 shows such a system with three states and the possible transitions between them. Markov models assume that the frequency of transitions between states is constant, although this is not necessarily true in practice (Modarres, Kaminskiy, & Krivtsov, 1999).

Figure 10. Markov process with three states

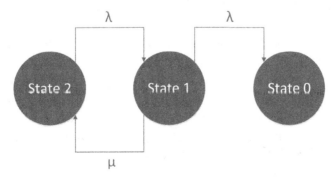

A stochastic process can be represented through a group states' description and their transition rate among states. According to the hypotheses assumed for the state transition specifications, the process is Markovian, semi-Markovian or non-Markovian. Although Markov method allows analysis of the exact failure probability, even when there are dependencies among components, it allows the integration of diverse kinds of knowledge to represent multi-state variables. However, modeling system which has a large number of variables becomes extremely complex. This complexity is a major problem in applying this method since there is a combinatory explosion of the states, which leads to difficulties in understanding the model for the modeling real system with a large number of variables (Weber, Medina-Oliva, Simon, & Iung, 2012).

Verma et al. (2011) pointed out the applicability of Markov models for modeling and evaluation of system aiming to assess dependability and system performance prior to implementation as a way to reduce the risk and cost of implementation. On the other hand, they identified the problem of increasing the complexity of the model with the number of variables as a disadvantage of this method. In addition to this lack, they noted that system, in some cases, lose his real form in the modeling process as well. In addition, some modelers have problems in converting the original system in the Markov model (Verma et al., 2011).

REAL WORLD CASES

The Struggle to Keep Pace With a Fast-Changing IT Environment

IDG White Paper, 2016

An IDG Research Services survey identifies several positive trends, including increasing IT budgets and cloud/outsourcing benefits. However, IT executives are facing challenges that range from unmet technology expectations to the growth of shadow IT. In this environment, IT executives and their departments are being asked to assume new responsibilities, to exploit emerging technologies, and to explore new organizational and IT deployment models. Simply talking about using IT to better support business goals is no longer enough; CIOs and other IT managers must deliver on that objective, and do so quickly. In its recent survey, IDG Research Services collected information from 140 CIOs and other IT executives and managers at U.S.-based organizations with at least 250 employees. Representing more than 15 different industry, government, and education sectors, the organizations averaged 9,200 employees and $518 million in annual revenues. Several basic necessities led the list of IT priorities, with maintaining system uptime and reliability topping the list. Other concerns, including disaster recovery and making data actionable, are more forward-looking and strategic. Available at: http://resources.idgenterprise.com/original/AST-0174328_CogecoIDGmpWP1014_UK.PDF

Cut Costs, Reduce Complexity, and Drive Availability for the Always-On Enterprise

IDC White Paper, March 2016

Businesses are now operating in a connected world, where customers, partners, and employees require constant access to data and applications through a wide variety of devices and online portals. Many businesses are currently executing digital transformation strategies to satisfy customer and employee demands for constant data access and availability. While they are modernizing their business processes through the use of IT, they find that they also need to modernize their datacenters to ensure the required speed and reliability to consistently deliver a great end-user experience. Datacenter modernization efforts are focused on 1) storage, to cater to the increased need for performance and availability while containing costs; 2) virtualization, to drive greater efficiency and automation; and 3) cloud, to create a more flexible and dynamic infrastructure. The goal for datacenter modernization, however, is to ensure the constant availability of all data and applications, which have become vital to business success. For businesses operating in this highly connected environment, downtime has become detrimental to business success, and the cost of downtime has skyrocketed. IDC estimates that the mean cost of one hour of downtime for an organization with between 1,000 and 4,999 employees is approximately $225,000. Consequently, businesses cannot tolerate the same levels of planned and unplanned downtime that they could before they started on their digital transformation journeys, and, for many businesses, the window for downtime is close to zero. Available at: http://www.cio.com.au/campaign/370984?content=%2Fwhitepaper%2F373 076%2Fcut-costs-reduce-complexity-and-drive-availability-for-the-always-on-enterprise%2F%3Ftype%3Dother%26arg%3D0%26location%3Drhs_related_whitepaper

CHAPTER SUMMARY

The main objective of this chapter was to provide the foundation of the concept of information system availability, determinants and measures as well as basics of system availability management. The chapter is composed of two parts. First, availability basics together with related terms (dependability, reliability and maintainability) are presented. Second, methods and techniques of system availability modeling are given with the brief description of: Reliability Block Diagrams, Fault Trees and Markov Chains.

Dependability is defined as property of a computer system such that reliance can justifiably be placed on the service it delivers. The service delivered by a system is its behavior as it is perceptible by its users who interacts with the system. User of the system can be human or another system. Concepts of dependability consists of three parts: the threats to, the attributes of, and the means by which dependability is attained. Reliability is the ability of a system or component to perform its required functions under stated conditions for a specified period of time. Maintainability is the system ability which measures the ease with which a software system or component can be modified to correct faults, improve performance or other attributes, or adapt to a changed environment. Availability can be defined as the degree to which a system or component is operational and accessible when required for use. Often expressed as a probability. It means that availability is a measure of the readiness of the system to be used when required for the purpose it was designed for. In general, availability is measured as the ratio of time in which the system was available in comparison to the total time of use. Different classifications of availability determinants are present in the literature, and it depends on the research approach and authors which classification will be used. Most common determinants in literature are presented in this chapter. System's manageability refers to the capability of a system to be managed and how easy the interaction with the system can be conducted.

A brief literature overview on the reliability and availability modeling is given in this section. In general, methods of availability modeling can be divided into three broader categories: analytical, quantitative and qualitative. Analytical methods use mathematical tools for modeling and simulation of services. In this chapter, Reliability Block Diagrams, Fault Trees and Markov Chains analytical methods are presented.

REFERENCES

Avižienis, A., Laprie, J.-C., & Randell, B. (2001). Fundamental Concepts of Computer System Dependability. *Proceedings of theIARP/IEEE-RAS Workshop on Robot Dependability: Technological Challenge of Dependable Robots in Human Environments,Seoul, Korea* (pp. 1–16).

Bajgoric, N. (2008). Continuous Computing Technologies for Enhancing Business Continuity. Hershey, PA: IGI Global.

Bajgoric, N., Spremic, M., & Turulja, L. (2011). Implementation of the IT governance standards through business continuity management: Cases from Croatia and Bosnia-Herzegovina. *Proceedings of the ITI 2011 33rd International Conference onInformation Technology Interfaces* (pp. 43–50).

Bauer, E. (2010). *Design for Reliability: Information and Computer-Based Systems*. John Wiley & Sons, Inc.

Bauer, E., Adams, R., & Eustace, D. (2011). *Beyond redundancy: how geographic redundancy can improve service availability and reliability of computer-based systems*. John Wiley & Sons, Inc. doi:10.1002/9781118104910

Bayram, S., Kirlidog, M., & Vayvay, O. (2010). Always-On Enterprise Information Systems with Service Oriented Architecture and Load Balancing. In N. Bajgoric (Ed.), Always-On Enterprise Information Systems for Business Continuance: Technologies for Reliable and Scalable Operations. Hershey, PA: IGI Global. doi:10.4018/978-1-60566-723-2.ch006

Birolini, A. (2014). *Reliability Engineering* (7th ed.). Springer Verlag. doi:10.1007/978-3-642-39535-2

Bodin, L. D., Gordon, L. A., & Loeb, M. P. (2005). Evaluting Information Security Investments Using the Analytic Hierarchy Process. *Communications of the ACM*, *48*(2), 79–83. doi:10.1145/1042091.1042094

Bodin, L. D., Gordon, L. A., & Loeb, M. P. (2008). Information Security and Risk Management. *Communications of the ACM*, *51*(4), 64–68. doi:10.1145/1330311.1330325

Cai, Z. (2008). Risk-Based Proactive Availability Management - Attaining High Performance and Resilience With Dynamic Self-Management. In *Enterprise Distributed Systems*. Georgia Institute of Technology.

Calzolari, F. (2006). *High availability using virtualization*. Universita di Pisa.

Chen, P., Kataria, G., & Krishnan, R. (2011). Correlated failures, diversification, and information security risk management. *Management Information Systems Quarterly, 35*(2), 397–422.

Clark, P. (2010). Contingency planning and strategies. *Proceedings of the2010 Information Security Curriculum Development Conference on Information Security Curriculum Development InfoSecCD '10.* doi:10.1145/1940941.1940969

CMMI. (2010). *CMMI for Services, Version 1.3 CMMI-SVC, V1.3 Improving processes for providing better services* (Vol. 520). Carnegie Mellon University.

Cocchiara, R. (2007). Beyond disaster recovery: becoming a resilient business (white paper). *IBM.*

Courtois, P.-J. (2008). *Justifying the Dependability of Computer-based Systems: With Applications in Nuclear Engineering.* Springer Science & Business Media.

Doguc, O. (2010). *Applications of Bayesian networks in complex system reliability.* Stevens Institute of Technology.

Faisst, U., & Prokein, O. (2008). Management of Security Risks - A Controlling Model for Banking Companies. In D. Seese, C. Weinhardt, & F. Schlottmann (Eds.), *Handbook on Information Technology in Finance* (pp. 73–93). Springer Berlin Heidelberg. doi:10.1007/978-3-540-49487-4_4

Fenton, N. (2012). *Risk Assessment and Decision Analysis with Bayesian Networks.* CRC Press.

Franke, U., Johnson, P., König, J., & Marcks von Würtemberg, L. (2012). Availability of enterprise IT systems: An expert-based Bayesian framework. *Software Quality Journal, 20*(2), 369–394. doi:10.1007/s11219-011-9141-z

Gay, S. C. (2007). An examination of virtualization's role in contingency planning. *Proceedings of the 4th annual conference on Information security curriculum development InfoSecCD '07.* doi:10.1145/1409908.1409927

Goyal, A., & Lavenberg, S. S. (1987). Modeling and analysis of computer system availability. *IBM Journal of Research and Development, 31*(6), 651–664. doi:10.1147/rd.316.0651

Grottke, M., Sun, H., Fricks, R. M., & Trivedi, K. S. (2008). Ten Fallacies of Availability and Reliability Analysis. *Proceedings of the 5th international conference on Service availability ISAS'08,* Tokyo (pp. 187–206). doi:10.1007/978-3-540-68129-8_15

Harper, M., Lawler, C., & Thornton, M. (2005). IT Application Downtime, Executive Visibility and Disaster Tolerant Computing. *Proceedings of the2nd International Conference on Cybernetics and Information Technologies, Systems and Applications.*

Harris, R., & Grimalla, M. (2008). Information Technology Contingency Planning. *Proceedings of the Southern Association for Information Systems Conference.*

Ibrahimovic, S., & Bajgoric, N. (2015). Modeling Information System Availability by Using Bayesian Belief Network Approach. Proceedings of the ENTerprise REsearch InNOVAtion Conference 2015, Kotor.

IEEE. (1990). *IEEE Software Glossary of Software Engineering Terminology.*

Immonen, A., & Niemelä, E. (2007). Survey of reliability and availability prediction methods from the viewpoint of software architecture. *Software & Systems Modeling, 7*(1), 49–65. doi:10.1007/s10270-006-0040-x

Ioannidis, C., Pym, D., & Williams, J. (2009). Investments and Trade-offs in the Economics of Information Security Presentation and Suggestions for Future Directions. *Proceedings of theInternational Conference on Financial Cryptography and Data Security* (*Vol. 2009*, pp. 148–166). Springer. doi:10.1007/978-3-642-03549-4_9

ISO/IEC. (2012). *ISO/IEC 27000.*

Laprie, J., Randell, B., Landwehr, C., & Member, S. (2004). *Basic Concepts and Taxonomy of Dependable and Secure Computing. IEEE Transactions on Dependable and Secure Computing, 1*(1), 11–33.

Laprie, J., & Roche, C. (1995). Dependability of Computer Systems: Concepts, Limits, Improvements. *Proceedings of theIEEE International Symposium on Fault-Tolerant Computing,* Pasadena, CA, USA (pp. 2–11). doi:10.1109/ISSRE.1995.497638

Liu, D., Deters, R., & Yhang, W. J. (2009). Architectural Design for Resilience Dong. *Enterprise Information Systems.*

Malek, M., Milic, B., & Milanovic, N. (2008). Analytical Availability Assessment of IT Services. *Proceedings of the 5th International Service Availability Symposium*. doi:10.1007/978-3-540-68129-8_16

Marcus, E., & Stern, H. (2003). Blueprints for high availability (2nd ed.). Indianapolis, IN, USA: John Wiley {&} Sons, Inc.

Martin, A. P., & Khazanci, D. (2006). Information Availability and Security Policy. *Proceedings of the Twelfth Americas Conference on Information Systems*.

Matthiesen, E. V., Hamouda, O., Ka, M., & Aniche Schwefel, H.-P. (2008). Dependability Evaluation of a Replication Service for Mobile Applications in Dynamic Ad-Hoc Networks. *Proceedings of the 5th International Service Availability Symposium*. doi:10.1007/978-3-540-68129-8_14

Milanovic, N. (2010). *Models, Methods and Tools for Availability Assessment of IT-Services and Business Processes*. Technidsche Universitat Berlin.

Modarres, M., Kaminskiy, M., & Krivtsov, V. (1999). *Reliability Engineering and Risk Analysis. Technometrics*. Marcel Dekker.

Morency, J. P., & Witty, R. J. (2011). *Hype cycle for business continuity management and it disaster recovery management, 2011. Technical report*. Gartner.

Pandey, M. (2000). *Fault tree analysis. Hazard Analysis Te.chniques for System*. University of Waterloo.

Raderius, J., Narman, P., & Ekstedt, M. (2009). Assessing system availability using an enterprise architecture analysis approach. *Proceedings of theInternational Conference on Service-Oriented Computing* (pp. 351-362). Springer. doi:10.1007/978-3-642-01247-1_36

Schiesser, R. (2010). *IT systems management*. Pearson Education, Inc.

Scott, D. (1999). *Making Smart Investments to Reduce Unplanned Downtime Unplanned*.

Singh, J. (2009). Modeling application availability. *Proceedings of the 2009 Spring Simulation Multiconference* (pp. 1–4).

Somasundaram, G., Shrivastava, A., & EMCEducation Services (Eds.). (2009). *Information Storage and Management: Storing, Managing, and Protecting Digital Information*. Wiley Publishing, Inc.

Tambe, S., Balasubramanian, J., Gokhale, A., & Damiano, T. (2007). MD-DPro: Model-Driven Dependability Provisioning in Enterprise Distributed Real-Time and Embedded Systems. *Proceedings of the4th International Service Availability Symposium.* doi:10.1007/978-3-540-72736-1_11

Taylor, M., Iqbal, M., & Nieves, M. (2007). *ITIL v3. Service Strategy.* Office of Government Commerce.

Tokuno, K., & Yamada, S. (2000). Markovian software availability measurement based on the number of restoration actions. *IEICE Transactions on Fundamentals, E83*(5), 835–841.5

Tokuno, K., & Yamada, S. (2008). User-Perceived Software Service Availability Modeling with Reliability Growth. *Proceedings of the5th International Service Availability Symposium.* doi:10.1007/978-3-540-68129-8_8

Trivedi, K., Ciardo, G., Dasarathy, B., Grottke, M., Rindos, A., & Vashaw, B. (2008). Achieving and Assuring High Availability. *Proceedings of the 5th International Service Availability Symposium* (pp. 1–7). doi:10.1109/IPDPS.2008.4536147

Troger, P., Feinbube, L., & Werner, M. (2016). WAP: What activates a bug? A refinement of the Laprie terminology model. *Proceedings of the 2015 IEEE 26th International Symposium on Software Reliability Engineering ISSRE '15* (pp. 106–111).

Verma, A. K., Ajit, S., & Kumar, M. (2011). Dependability of networked computer-based Systems.*Proc. of 3rd Information Survivability Workshop.* Springer-Verlag.

Weber, P., Medina-Oliva, G., Simon, C., & Iung, B. (2012). Overview on Bayesian networks applications for dependability, risk analysis and maintenance areas. *Engineering Applications of Artificial Intelligence, 25*(4), 671–682. doi:10.1016/j.engappai.2010.06.002

Chapter 2
IT Governance Standards and Regulations

INTRODUCTION

Besides the economic aspect which affects the level of investment in IT infrastructure, from the standpoint of system availability, there are regulations that require some security controls in many industries. These regulations require investments in IT infrastructure even in cases when there is no economic justification but have a positive effect on raising the availability of IT systems.

For instance, IT systems in financial institutions are subject of regular audits by independent auditing companies which mostly rely on international standards for the management of IT systems. This is the indirect way of setting the requirements to align IT systems of financial institutions with these standards. It happens that the implementation of certain requirement of these standards has no economic justification, but its implementation reduces the risks of IS and increases system availability. An overview of some regulations and standards that banks must be in compliance with and that have direct impact on implementation of controls that improve system availability will be given in this chapter.

This chapter is composed of two parts: the first part presents the standards that are directly related to financial institutions and refer exclusively to them (Basel II and the payment card industry data security standard); second part considers standards for IS security management in general and can be applied on firms in all industries (ITIL, COBIT, ISO/IEC 27001:2013). Karkoskova

DOI: 10.4018/978-1-5225-2268-3.ch002

& Feuerlicht (2015) pointed out that ITIL and COBIT have similar objectives that include maximizing return on Investment, value creation, and IT investment optimization, leading to achievement of competitive advantage by using advanced IT technologies.

STANDARDS AND REGULATIONS FOR FINANCIAL INSTITUTIONS

Basel II

Basel II is a set of regulations adopted by the Basel Committee on Banking Supervision (hereinafter referred to as the Committee) which regulates the size of the bank's capital relative to risk exposure. Basel II regulations are related to internationally active banks from the countries members of G10[1]. The European Union has passed a directive (CAD3) that the provisions of the agreement became mandatory for all banks in the EU countries since the beginning of 2007.

According to the Basel II agreement, banks have to provide capital to cover expected losses on operational risk. Operational risk is the risk of loss resulting from inadequate or failed internal processes, people, systems or external events. This definition includes legal risk, but excludes strategic and reputational risk (Basel Committee on Banking Supervision, 2001). Security risks are a subset of operational risk. Figure 1 provides a classification of the loss event by type according to Basel II and BSI, which portrays that security risk are included in a large number of categories of operational risk.

Recognizing the specificity of electronic banking risk as well as its importance, the Committee issued a document "Risk Management Principles for Electronic Banking", which deals with this issue. In this document, e-banking is defined as "the provision of retail and small value banking products and services through electronic channels as well as large value electronic payments and other wholesale banking services delivered electronically". The document listed the following factors that may affect the risk management:

- The speed of change relating to technological and customer service innovation in e-banking is unprecedented. In order to efficiently maintain that pace, it is necessary for management to ensure adequate strategic assessment, risk analysis and security reviews are conducted prior to implementing new e-banking applications.

Figure 1. Loss event type classification according to BSI
Source: Faisst & Prokein (2006)

Loss Event Type Classification
according to Basel II

Loss Event Type Classification according to BSI	Internal fraud	External fraud	Business disruption and system failures	Clients, products & business practicess	Damage to physical assets	Employment practices and workplace safety	Execution delivery & process management
Act of nature beyond control					e.g. fire		
Organizational deficiencies			e.g. insufficient maintanace				e.g. insufficient net capacity
Deliberate act	e.g. theft of hardware	e.g. theft of data	e.g. computer virus	e.g. misuse of confidental information	e.g. terror attack		
Human error	e.g. careless erasure of objects		e.g. server switch-off in going concern		e.g. negligent demolition of hardware		e.g. incorrect data input
Technical failure			e.g. breakdown of electric power supply				e.g. server failure

- E-banking products are generally integrated with the "core" banking applications. In this way, possibility of human error is reduced, but at the same time increases dependence on sound systems design and architecture as well as system interoperability and operational scalability.
- E-banking increases bank's is dependence on information technologies leading to the emergence of new partnerships with companies such as ISP providers, telecom operators and others, which carry additional operational and security risks.
- The openness of the Internet as a global network that can be accessed without restrictions, from any place, routing of messages through unknown locations are additional risks to the security of information and customer privacy standards.

The Committee has therefore published a set of 14 principles divided into three categories which cover the area of e-banking services to help banks to better manage risk associated with e-banking:

- Board and Management Oversight (Principles 1 to 3);
- Security Controls (Principles 4 to 10); and
- Legal and Reputational Risk Management (Principles 11 to 14).

These principles are as follows:

1. The Board of Directors and senior management should establish effective management oversight over the risks associated with e-banking activities, including the establishment of specific accountability, policies and controls to manage these risks.
2. The Board of Directors and senior management should review and approve the key aspects of the bank's security control process.
3. The Board of Directors and senior management should establish a comprehensive and ongoing due diligence and oversight process for managing the bank's outsourcing relationships and other third-party dependencies supporting e- banking.
4. Banks should take appropriate measures to authenticate the identity and authorization of customers with whom it conducts business over the Internet.
5. Banks should use transaction authentication methods that promote non-repudiation and establish accountability for e-banking transactions.
6. Banks should ensure that appropriate measures are in place to promote adequate segregation of duties within e-banking systems, databases and applications.
7. Banks should ensure that proper authorization controls and access privileges are in place for e-banking systems, databases and applications.
8. Banks should ensure that appropriate measures are in place to protect the data integrity of e-banking transactions, records and information.
9. Banks should ensure that clear audit trails exist for all e-banking transactions.
10. Banks should take appropriate measures to preserve the confidentiality of key e-banking information. Measures taken to preserve confidentiality should be commensurate with the sensitivity of the information being transmitted and/or stored in databases.
11. Banks should ensure that adequate information is provided on their websites to allow potential customers to make an informed conclusion about the bank's identity and regulatory status of the bank prior to entering into e-banking transactions.
12. Banks should take appropriate measures to ensure adherence to customer privacy requirements applicable to the jurisdictions to which the bank is providing e-banking products and services.
13. Banks should have effective capacity, business continuity and contingency planning processes to help ensure the availability of e-banking systems and services.

14. Banks should develop appropriate incident response plans to manage, contain and minimize problems arising from unexpected events, including internal and external attacks, that may hamper the provision of e-banking systems and services (Basel Committee on Banking Supervision Risk, 2003).

It should be noted that these are not requirements that banks must meet or even best practice because the Committee recognized that the profile of e-banking risk is different for each bank. Therefore, each bank should have its own program for managing the risks associated with e-banking.

The Payment Card Industry Data Security Standard

PCI DSS was developed by the Council of several financial institutions in order to improve data security in payment systems. It includes guidelines for user authentication, firewalls, anti-virus measures, and more. The PCI Security Standards Council is open global forum for the ongoing development, enhancement, storage, distribution and implementation of security standards for protecting accounts information. The mission of the Council is to improve data security in payment systems through education and raising awareness of the PCI Security Standards. PCI council was established in 2006 and consists of representatives of companies American Express, Discover Financial Services, JCB International, MasterCard Worldwide and Visa Inc. PCI DSS is a comprehensive security standard that includes requirements for security management, policies, procedures, network architecture, software design and other critical protective measures. This comprehensive standard is intended to help organizations with proactive protection of customer account data. The PCI Security Standards Council will enhance the PCI DSS as needed to ensure that the standard includes any new or modified requirements necessary to mitigate emerging payment security risks, while continuing to foster wide-scale adoption. Feedback from the Advisory Committee and other participating organizations is taken into account during the development of standards. All key players are encouraged to contribute to the creation of proposals for additions or changes to the PCI DSS. The core of the PCI DSS is a group of principles and accompanying requirements, around which the specific elements of the DSS are organized:

Each bank and other institutions dealing with the transactions of payment cards are required to meet the requirements of PCI DSS and, if required, to hold a certificate that confirms compatibility with PCI DSS.

Table 1. PCI DSS Requirements

Element	Requirement
Build and Maintain a Secure Network	Install and maintain a firewall configuration to protect cardholder data.
	Do not use vendor-supplied defaults for system passwords and other security parameters.
Protect Cardholder Data	Protect stored cardholder data.
	Encrypt transmission of cardholder data across open, public networks.
Maintain a Vulnerability Management Program	Use and regularly update anti-virus software.
	Develop and maintain secure systems and applications.
Implement Strong Access Control Measures	Restrict access to cardholder data by business need-to-know.
	Restrict access to cardholder data by business need-to-know.
	Restrict physical access to cardholder data.
Regularly Monitor and Test Networks	Track and monitor all access to network resources and cardholder data.
	Regularly test security systems and processes.
Maintain an Information Security Policy	Maintain a policy that addresses information security.

Source: Kouns & Minoli (2010), p. 279

STANDARDS FOR IS SECURITY MANAGEMENT

There are several standards and sets of recommendations which define the best way to manage IT functions of the company. Some of the standards that deal with information security management are:

- ITIL (Information Technology Infrastructure Library) is a set of practices for IT service management that focuses on aligning IT services with the needs of business issued by the UK Office of Government Commerce.
- COBIT (Control Objectives for Information and related Technology) is issued by ISACA (Information Systems Audit and Control Association) and created as a framework which should establish a control link between IT processes and business requirements. Other management parts are added to COBIT during its further development making it a complete framework for the management of the IT function.
- ISO/IEC 27001: 2013 (The Code of Practice for Information Security Management) is the international standard for information security management.

- ISO/IEC TR 1335 (Guidelines for the Management of IT Security) is a technical document that provides information and guidance on IT security both from the control and the implementation perspective.
- ISO/IEC 15408 (Security Techniques Evaluation Criteria for IT Security) is used as a reference for the review and certification of IT products and services security.
- TickITis issued by the British Standards Institute. It is used for evaluation and certification of quality management software. The basic idea of TickIT is that the quality is a part of the software development process and that quality goals have to be achieved during development process. This standard can be used in conjunction with ISO 9001 for the processes of software development. The application of this standard can significantly reduce operational risk caused by bad software development.
- NIST (National Institute of Standards and Technology) is established by The Computer Security Resource Center (CSRC), which deals with the security of information systems and issues standards and recommendations for information security.
- Internal Control-Integrated Framework issued by COSO and offering the framework whose application should improve the process of financial reporting by improving the internal control processes. Internal controls that lead to reduction of operational risks associated with IT function are defined by this document.

It should be noted that one of the biggest risks that IT can bring to contemporary bank is inadequate use of the opportunities which are result of constant improvements of IT, and consequently reduce the competitiveness of the bank. Therefore, from the standpoint of risk, it is necessary to observe the management of IT operations as a whole, and information security management is only part of that. For this reason, standards that consider IT function as a whole, ITIL and COBIT, together with ISO 27001: 2013, will be described in the following section.

ITIL –ISO/IEC20000

ITIL considers all elements of organizations' IT function, but from the perspective of this book, it is particularly interesting because of the approach in managing the availability. In particular, ITIL is the source for a large numbers of the best practices on the determinants of availability.

ITIL is a set of concepts and policies for managing IT infrastructure, development and operations. The development of ITIL started in the eighties of the twentieth century at the request of the British Government, by Central Computer & Telecommunication Agency as a response to the growing dependence on information technology and the increasing complexity of IT systems. ITIL v1 was published between 1989 and 1996 in the form of a collection of more than 30 books. In 2000, the UK Office of Government Commerce released ITIL v2 as a set of eight books, each covering a specific topic of IT management. Although simplified, ITIL2 has been criticized as too confusing and complex. In response to criticism, ITIL3 was released in 2007. ITIL3 reduced the number of publications on five: service strategy, service design, service transition, service operation, and continual service improvement. The enhanced version of ITIL3 was published in 2011.

ISO/IEC20000 is an international standard for quality assurance of IT services - IT services management. By implementing the requirements defined by this standard, the organization introduces the system of IT services management which can be certified under the same norms to provide proof of the quality of IT services. It has almost completely taken over all the ITIL terminology and scope so ITIL can be considered as *de facto* standard, since the ISO 20000 is the only valid standard for IT service management today (Spremić & Kostić, 2008). However, it is important to note that ITIL could not be implemented, but organization can benefit from a variety of recommendations and best practices contained in it. ITIL is a set of best practices for IT service management that emphasize the central role of service users. ITIL is published in a number of books which cover various areas of IT management services. This section provides a brief overview of all modules with a little more extensive attention to security management.

The main tasks to which is ITIL dedicated to are:

- Operation and maintenance of the existing system;
- Development of the new system; and
- Constant adaptation in order to provide services according to the changing demands of business.

ITIL framework is based on the five stages of the life cycle of services: service strategy, service design, service transition, service operation, and continual service improvement. In the center of this life cycle is a service strategy, followed by the service design, service transition, and service operation. Continual service improvement (CSI) surrounds and supports all phases of the life cycle. Both phases influence each other and are mutually

Figure 2. ITIL life cycle
Source: TSO report, 2007

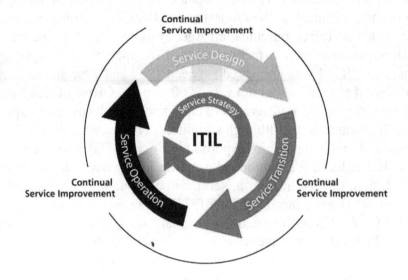

supportive in terms of input and output information. The purpose of CSI life cycle is to align IT services to changing business needs by identifying and implementing improvements to IT services that support business processes (Taylor, 2007).

Service Strategy

At the core of the service lifecycle is service strategy. Service Strategy provides guidance on how to set service management not only as an organizational capability but as a strategic asset. Guidance is provided on the principles underpinning the practice of service management which are useful for developing service management policies, guidelines and processes across the ITIL Service Lifecycle. Topics covered in service strategy include the development of service markets, characteristics of internal and external provider types, service assets, the service portfolio and implementation of strategy through the Service Lifecycle. Financial management, demand management, organizational development and strategic risks are among other major topics.

Organizations should use the guidelines of service strategy to set goals and expectations about the performance of services provided, and to identify, select and prioritize opportunities. The problem that service strategy solves is to ensure that organizations are able to manage the costs and risks associated with their portfolio of services, and that services are set up to ensure not only operational efficiency, but also to achieve high performance (TSO report, 2007).

Service Design

Service design is the stage in the life cycle that turns service strategy into plan for delivering the business goals. Service design provides guidance for the design and development of services and service management practices. It covers the principles and methods for transforming strategic objectives into portfolio of services. The scope of service design is not limited to new services but it includes the changes and improvements that need to be done in order to increase or maintain the values that are delivered to customers over the life cycle of services, the continuity of services, achievement the agreed level of service, as well as compliance with standards and regulations. Among the key issues covered by service design are: service catalogue, availability, capacity, continuity and service level management (TSO report, 2007).

Service Transition

Service transition provides guidance for the development and improvement of capabilities for transitioning new and changed services into a production operation. It provides guidance on how the requirements of service strategy encoded in the service design are effectively implemented through a phase of service operation by controlling the risks of failure and disruption. It combines practices in change, configuration, asset management, commissioning and implementation, program, risk management and places them in the practical context of service management. It provides guidance on the management of complexity which comes as a result of changes in services and process management services; provides guidance on how to prevent undesired events that occur during the introduction of innovations (TSO report, 2007).

Service Operation

Service operation provides guidance on the practices in the management of the day-to-day operation of services. It includes guidance on achieving effectiveness and efficiency in delivery and support of services in order to ensure value for the customer and the service provider. The strategic objectives in the end are achieved through the service operation, which makes this phase of crucial phase in the life cycle of services. Instructions are related to the manner of maintaining stability in the service operation, while allowing changes in design, scale, scope and level of services. Among the topics in this document are event, incident, problem, request, application and technical management practices and it discusses some of the newer industry practices to manage virtual and service-oriented architectures (TSO report, 2007).

Continual Service Improvement

Continuous service improvement provides instrumental guidance in creating and maintaining value for customers through better design, transition and operation of services. These recommendations combine the principles, practices and methods from quality management, change management and capability improvement. Organizations can learn how to realize incremental and large-scale improvements in service quality, operational efficiency and business continuity. Instructions are related to the linking of efforts and outcomes in improving the strategy, design and transition. A closed loop based on the Plan-Do-Check-Act (PDCA) model presented in Figure 2 is established and capable of receiving inputs for the improvement of any planning perspective (TSO report, 2007). Quality cycle is used in the structure of the practices in each of the core guides of ITIL, i.e. the ITIL framework incorporates the Deming Quality Cycle by applying it to the Service Lifecycle stages that helps align the practices of ITIL to the structure of external practices such as COBIT.

Figure 3 illustrates the reach of each of the governance and operational elements across the lifecycle. It is important to note that the ITIL is widely accepted and its principles form the basis for other vendor-related standards (e.g. HP ITSM and Microsoft Operations Framework -MOF).

The goal of incident management is to restore service to normal operation as quickly as possible and to reduce the negative impact on the business, ensuring the maintenance of the best possible levels of service quality and availability. The goal of problem management is to prevent problems and resulting incidents from happening, to eliminate recurring incidents and to minimize the impact of incidents that cannot be prevented. Problem management differs from incident management because the primary purpose of problem management is find and fix the cause of the problem and prevent the incident, and the purpose of incident management is to restore service to the level defined by Service Level Agreement (SLA) as soon as possible, with the least possible impact on the business. Service level management provides continuous identification, monitoring and review of the level of IT services specified in SLA. In addition, it ensures written agreements with

Figure 3. The Deming Quality Cycle
Source: TSO report, 2007, p.13

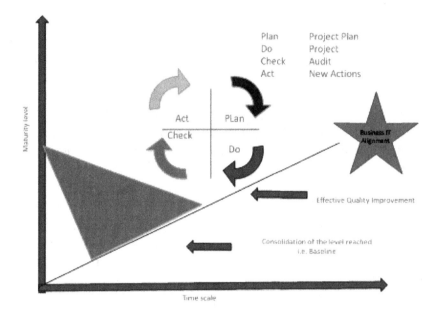

Figure 4. Service Lifecycle governance and operational elements
Source: TSO report, 2007, p.150

Service Lifestyle Governance Processes		Service Lifestyle Operational Processes			
Continual Service Improvement Processes	Service Strategy Processes	Service Design Processes	Service Transition Processes	Service Operation Processes	
Service Measurement	Demand Management				
	Strategy Generation				
	Service Portfolio Management				
	IT Financial Management				
		Service Catalogue Management			
		Service Level Management			
		Capacity Management			
		Availability Management			
		Service Continuity Management			
Service Reporting	Information Security Management				
	Supplier Management				
			Transition Planning and Support		
	Change Management				
	Service Asset and Configuration Management				
			Release and Development Management		
			Service Validation and Testing		
			Evaluation		
Service Improvement	Knowledge Management				
				Event Management	
				Incident Management	
				Request Fulfilment	
				Problem Management	
				Access Management	
				Operation Management	

the internal IT departments and external suppliers on the service level targets and responsibilities within SLAs and SLRs (Service Level Agreements and Service Level Requirements). Capacity management is closely related to operational processes in order to control their activities. The main role of the capacity management is to establish a set of measures to monitor the service and their evaluation in relation to the default values. The goal of change management is to ensure that standardized methods and procedures are used for the effective implementation of all changes. Change is an event that results in a new status of one or more components of the system. It must be approved by management and it takes into account the efficient use of resources. Changes should improve or repair business process with minimal risk to the IT infrastructure. IT service continuity management (ITSCM) encompasses the planning and management in order to ensure the required IT systems and technologies can be resumed within required timescale, even after a serious incident happens. These processes include not only a set of reactive measures, but proactive measures for disaster risk reduction as well. Finally, availability management should ensures the agreed level of availability is provided. Availability management should look to continually optimize and improve availability of the IT infrastructure, the services and supporting organization. The main goal of these actions is to deliver business and customer benefits (TSO report, 2007).

COBIT

COBIT (Control Objectives for Information and related Technology) can generally be described as a set of best practices for the management, control and audit of IT systems. COBIT considers IT systems management as an inseparable part of the management of the entire organization. As a part of such a system, IT system management is subject of a constant process of quality management which consists of four steps: plan, do, check, act (the same as ITIL and Quality Cycle presented in Figure 2). COBIT is developed by ISACA - Information System Audit & Control Association in 1999.

In order for an organization to adequately manage the information, it must satisfy quality, safety and regulatory requirements. At the same time, management has to optimize the use of available resources including data, hardware, software, communications resources, facilities and people. To successfully address these two tasks, management must understand the status of its own IT systems and decide which measures should be established. COBIT framework offers guidelines that help management to solve the tasks bridging the gap between business risks, control needs and technical issues. The solutions presented in the COBIT framework are agreed at the expert level, helping to optimize IT investments and provide measurability that provides gradation.

COBIT has 37 high-level control objectives, one for each IT process. Therefore, it is possible to verify if adequate control system is implemented in a specific IT system by verification of the COBIT control objectives. COBIT guidelines for management provide a link between IT control and IT governance. These guidelines are general and contain guidelines for: controlling of information and processes for information management in the organization, monitoring the status of the organization's objectives, monitoring and improving the performance of each IT process as well as benchmarking of organization's achievements. Using these guidelines, management can get answers to questions such as:

- How far to go in controlling IS and whether control outcomes justify the costs?
- What are the key performance indicators?
- What are the key success factors?
- What are the risks if we do not meet the objectives?
- What others do?
- How to measure and compare the maturity of the organization with respect to best practices?
- What is the strategy for improvement?

COBIT IT processes, business requirements and detailed control objectives define what needs to be done in order to implement an adequate control structure. Guidelines for the control contain additional detailed instructions intended for people who carry out the implementation to be able to implement specific controls based on analysis of operational and IT risks. In order to achieve the objectives set out in the organization, COBIT provides constant revision procedures. Guidelines for auditing include activities to be implemented during the audit for each of the 37 control objectives.

Implementation guidance contains a methodology for the implementation and development of IT management functions using COBIT. This guide focuses on the generic methodology for the implementation of IT management and covers the following areas:

- The importance of managing IT functions and reasons for implementation;
- Lifecycle of IT management function;
- COBIT framework;

- Relationship between COBIT and program of IT function management;
- A list of people interested in the program of IT function management;
- Plan to implement a program of IT governance using COBIT.

COBIT 5 has 37 high level processes in five domains presented in Figure 5:

- Evaluate, Deliver and Monitor (EDM);
- Align, Plan and Organize (APO);
- Build, Acquire and Implement (BAI);
- Deliver, Service and Support (DSS); and
- Monitor, Evaluate and Assess (MEA).

COBIT provides that information to be used in business should meet the following criteria:

- **Quality Requirements:**
  - **Effectiveness:** The relevance and pertinence of information to the business process as well as the timely, correct, consistent, and usable delivery.
  - **Efficiency:** The provision of information through the optimum use of resources.
- **Security Requirements:**
  - **Confidentiality:** The protection of sensitive information from unauthorized disclosure.
  - **Integrity:** The accuracy and completeness of information, as well as its validity, in accordance with business values and expectations.
  - **Availability:** Information being available when required by the business process now and in the future. It also concerns the safeguarding of necessary resources and associated capabilities.
- **Fiduciary Requirements:**
  - **Compliance:** Deals with following those laws, regulations, and contractual arrangements to which the business process is subject.
  - **Reliability:** Relates to the provision of appropriate information for management to operate the entity and for management to exercise its financial and compliance-reporting responsibilities.

Function of IT management is a daily work based on periodic measurements of a degree of defined standards and take appropriate and timely remedial action that should eliminate the deviation. The biggest advantage of COBIT is in its prescribing metrics for managing the IT function.

Figure 5. COBIT's processes
Source: ISACA

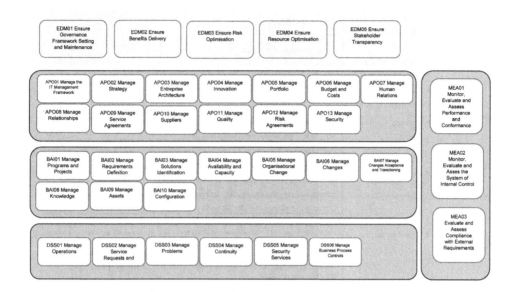

ISO/IEC 27001:2013

ISO/IEC 27001:2013 is international standard for information security management known as the "Code of Practice for Information Security Management". ISO/IEC 27001:2013 consists of 127 controls grouped into 10 areas. These controls are based on the experience and best practices and most of these controls are suitable for implementation in any organization regardless of size and type.

ISO/IEC 27001:2013 was developed based on BS7799 standard (British Standards Institute). Complement this standard is ISO/IEC 27001:2013 gives the specification of the system for managing information security (Information Security Management System - ISMS).

ISO/IEC 27001:2013 has the following sections, as shown in Figure 6:

- **Introduction:** The standard uses a process approach.
- **Scope:** It specifies generic ISMS requirements suitable for organizations of any type, size or nature.
- **Normative References:** Only ISO/IEC 27000 is considered absolutely essential to users of 27001: the remaining ISO27k standards are optional.

Figure 6. ISO/IEC 27001:2013 Main Sections
Source: ISO

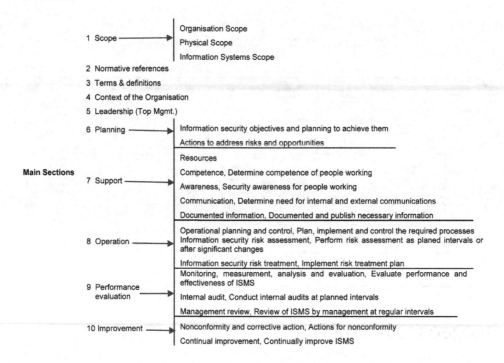

- **Terms and Definitions:** A brief, formalized glossary, soon to be superseded by ISO/IEC 27000.
- **Context of the Organization:** Understanding the organizational context, the needs and expectations of interested parties, and defining the scope of the ISMS.
- **Leadership:** Top management must demonstrate leadership and commitment to the ISMS, mandate policy, and assign information security roles, responsibilities and authorities.
- **Planning:** Outlines the process to identify, analyze and plan to treat information risks, and clarify the objectives of information security.
- **Support:** Adequate, competent resources must be assigned, awareness raised, documentation prepared and controlled.
- **Operation:** A bit more detail about assessing and treating information risks, managing changes, and documenting things.
- **Performance Evaluation:** Monitor, measure, analyze and evaluate the information security controls, processes and management system in order to make systematic improvements where appropriate.

- **Improvement:** Address the findings of audits and reviews, make continual refinements to the ISMS.
- **Annex A Reference Control Objectives and Controls:** Annex is normative, implying that certified organizations are expected to use it, but they are free to deviate from or supplement it in order to address their particular information risks.
- **Bibliography:** Points readers to five related standards, plus part 1 of the ISO/IEC directives, for more information. In addition, ISO/IEC 27000 is identified in the body of the standard as a normative standard and there are several references to ISO 31000 on risk management.

Although it is advisable for any organization to implement this standard, it is invaluable for financial institutions and banks. Many operational risks related to IT are covered by this standard, although the standard does not define control processes. Each organization is allowed to choose which control wants to implement and in what way to control their application. Therefore, this standard ideally complements the ISO/IEC 27002:2013 which deals with control of all the areas defined in ISO/IEC 27001:2013, making it possible to perform the compliance certification system for information security management with this standard.

REAL WORLD CASES

Reducing Downtime and Business Loss: Addressing Business Risk with Effective Technology, IDC White Paper, IDC, August (2009)

Business risk can appear at your company's doorstep at any time — and in many forms. Systems go offline when aging components fail, natural disasters strike, key networking connections don't work, or a local contractor cuts a power cable. Maintaining productive and smoothly running business operations is absolutely mission critical — and that is even more evident in today's challenging economic conditions. The critical components of an effective IT infrastructure — servers, storage, software, and all of the networking links — must be up and running, all the time, to maintain business momentum and employee productivity. In many small and even midsize businesses, current IT systems may not be up to date or easy to manage, and this situation sets the stage for potential problems down the road. IDC customer-based studies show that using appropriate technology in consistent ways helps small and medium-sized (SMB) organizations, even as they address changing requirements. As discussed in the following pages, IDC research with leading SMBs shows that well-targeted technology upgrades, coupled with a rigorous program to standardize and improve IT practices, can deliver substantial risk reduction and could reduce total annual outage risk by as much as 85%, in some cases, with downtime reduced from an average of over 2 hours per month to less than 45 minutes. By adopting industry best practices compliance regulations (e.g., ITIL, CobiT), companies can lower annual downtime by up to 85%, greatly reducing interruptions to daily data processing and access, supporting business continuity, and containing operational costs. Available at: http://www.compaq.net/hpinfo/newsroom/press_kits/2009/CompetitiveEdge/ReducingDowntime.pdf

COBIT Case Study: Gaining Control of IT with COBIT

The IT organization of X-Bank (original name withheld) was facing a great deal of challenges with day-to-day IT service delivery. While critical activities, such as end-of-day, backup and restore functions, and scheduled server reboot for certain critical servers were documented on paper for regulatory compliance reasons, most processes were at best documented in individual employees' heads. There was poor change control; something broke every other day and it was perfectly acceptable to have unplanned downtime of banking services for a few hours every month. Often, the unplanned downtime was due to, for example, failed system upgrades or security configuration modifications by the security administrators without proper impact assessments. Fortunately, the enterprise's internal control department had some oversight over the critical banking infrastructure; otherwise, banking operations could have suffered a total systemic failure. In the marketplace, relatively smaller banks were recording better performance and were perceived as more reputable than X-Bank. Within the bank, the business executives did not trust IT's ability to effectively and efficiently support business objectives, and IT was obviously overwhelmed with the challenges. Available at: http://www.isaca.org/Knowledge-Center/cobit/Pages/COBIT-Case-Study-Gaining-Control-of-IT-With-COBIT.aspx

COBIT Case Study: IT Risk Management in a Bank

The bank in the given case is a global conglomerate with operations in more than 50 countries and with more than 125,000 employees across the globe. The bank's technology teams are located throughout the world to support global lines of business. The IT teams include development centres that are part of the bank and others that are outsourced to vendors, as well as technology back offices that support IT infrastructure and services. The bank had a history of multiple governance and assurance templates and processes followed by different teams, regions and locations. Hence, the key challenge was to create a common governance and assurance process across technology teams. The technology governance and assurance programme was designed through a risk management framework to ensure effective risk and control management. Available at: http://www.isaca.org/Knowledge-Center/cobit/Pages/COBIT-Case-Study-IT-Risk-Management-in-a-Bank.aspx

CHAPTER SUMMARY

The main objective of this chapter was to provide the overview of regulations and standards that banks must be in compliance with and that have direct impact on implementation of controls that improve system availability. The chapter is composed of two parts. First, standards that are directly related to financial institutions and refer exclusively to them (Basel II and the payment card industry data security standard) are presented. Second, presentation of standards for IS security management in general that can be applied on firms in all industries (ITIL, COBIT, ISO/IEC 27001:2013) is given. In summary:

Basel II is a set of regulations adopted by the Basel Committee on Banking Supervision which regulates the size of the bank's capital relative to risk exposure. The Committee has published a set of 14 principles divided into three categories which cover the area of e banking services to help banks to better manage risk associated with e-banking.

The Payment Card Industry Data Security Standard - PCI DSS was developed by the Council of several financial institutions in order to improve data security in payment systems. It includes guidelines for user authentication, firewalls, anti-virus measures, and more. The PCI Security Standards Council is open global forum for the ongoing development, enhancement, storage, distribution and implementation of security standards for protecting accounts information.

ITIL is a set of concepts and policies for managing IT infrastructure, development and operations. The main tasks to which is ITIL dedicated to are: operation and maintenance of the existing system; development of the new system; constant adaptation in order to provide services according to the changing demands of business. ITIL framework is based on the five stages of the life cycle of services: service strategy, service design, service transition, service operation, and continual service improvement.

COBIT (Control Objectives for Information and related Technology) can generally be described as a set of best practices for the management, control and audit of IT systems. COBIT consider IT systems management as an inseparable part of the management of the entire organization. COBIT 5 has 37 high level processes in five domains.

ISO/IEC 27001:2013 is international standard for information security management known as the "Code of Practice for Information Security Management". ISO/IEC 27001:2013 consists of 127 controls grouped into 10 areas. These controls are based on the experience and best practices and most of these controls are suitable for implementation in any organization regardless of size and type.

REFERENCES

Faisst, U., & Prokein, O. (2008). Management of Security Risks - A Controlling Model for Banking Companies. In D. Seese, C. Weinhardt, & F. Schlottmann (Eds.), *Handbook on Information Technology in Finance* (pp. 73–93). Springer. doi:10.1007/978-3-540-49487-4_4

Karkoskova, S., & Feuerlicht, G. (2015). Extending MBI Model using ITIL and COBIT Processes. *Journal of Systems Integration*, 5, 29–44. doi:10.20470/jsi.v6i4.244

Kouns, J., & Minoli, D. (2010). *Information Technology Risk Management in Enterprise Environments: A Review of Industry Practices and A Practical Guide to Risk Management Teams.*

Spremić, M., & Kostić, D. (2008). Upravljanje kvalitetom informatičke usluge: Studije slučaja primjene ITIL metode. *Poslovna Izvrsnost*, 2(1), 37–58.

Taylor, S. (2007). *The Official Introduction to the ITIL Service Lifecycle*. London: The Stationary Office.

ENDNOTE

[1]   USA, Belgium, Canada, France, Japan, United Kingdom, Germany, Switzerland, Italy, Sweden, The Netherlands

Chapter 3
IT Infrastructure/IS Availability Investments and Optimization

INTRODUCTION

Organizations are making huge investments in information technology. As the spending on IT increases, the awareness on the IT returns is becoming significant. Organizations are concerned on how their money invested in IT can be returned as a value (Ahmad & Arshad, 2014). Previous researches have investigated the effects of IT on profitability, efficacy, value of the company etc. One of the results of prior research is so-called „*IT productivity paradox*" from 1990s, the term that explained paradox as a discrepancy of the advances in computer technology and the productivity of firms. It practically means the following: the increase in technology investment does not produce increase in productivity. However, although main reason for investments in IT was to increase productivity and efficacy in the 1990s, modern business has spawned many other reasons for these investments. Reasons have changed and investments in IT are today reflected in the organization's strategic planning for competitiveness and survival.. Ahmad & Arshad (2014) identified five major factors that describe the IT investment values to the organizations: financial, operational, organizational, strategic, and service values. Principally, the question of justification of IT investment as well as investment optimization is very interesting among both scholars

DOI: 10.4018/978-1-5225-2268-3.ch003

and practitioners. To select the optimal technical and organizational control that will be implemented in order to ensure system availability, investment should meet at least one of two criteria:

- To bring measurable financial benefits. In the case of investment in IS security, benefit is measured through avoidance of potential losses.
- There is a demand of regulatory bodies for the introduction of specific systems and technologies.

To estimate the financial benefit, it is necessary to predict the potential damage that may result from the failure of IT systems. Various mathematical models based on historical data can be used for prediction of the potential losses resulting from operational risks (including the risks related to the use of IT which presents the majority of operational risk in retail banks). Such models generally predict losses incurred as a result of events with great frequency because there is sufficient historical data base. However, a major problem of models based on historical data is the lack of data on small frequency events with a great influence on the business. As an adequate alternative, models based on probability have been developed. Bayesian Belief Networks are used as a tool for modeling in the field of information security and operational risks. Therefore, this chapter will provide brief overview of the literature regarding economic viability of investments in IS availability as well as seven methods for optimization of IT investments: return on investment, return on security investment, cost/benefit analysis, analytic hierarchy process, game theory, real options analysis, value at security risk.

ECONOMIC VIABILITY OF INVESTMENTS IN IS AVAILABILITY

Although a lot of work has been done on the economic viability of investments in information systems (Schniederjans, Hamaker, & Schniederjans, 2004; Hamaker, 2009; Bardhan & Sougstad, 2004; Serafeimidis, 1997; Kumar, 2004) and investment in security of information systems and thus indirectly the investment in system availability, few papers explicitly considered the economic viability of investments in system availability. Gordon & Loeb (2002) developed the first model to estimate the investment in information security as a basis for concluding that it is most profitable to invest in the protection and prevention of threats that have medium impact on the security of information.

One of the pioneers of this scientific area is Ross Anderson, who in 2001 explained the investment in information security using microeconomic concepts (Anderson, 2001). Also, along with Moore (Anderson & Moore, 2006), he gave an overview of research and open issues in this area. Bodin et al. (2005) proposed a model for optimal allocation of the budget to maintain and improve the security of information systems, based on the improved Analytic Hierarchy Process (AHP), as a tool for multi-criteria analysis. Gordon & Loeb (2006) developed a model based on the net present value of the investment, for the process of budgeting investment in information security. Ioannidis & Pym (2009) developed a model that considers investments in information security in terms of organization's preference towards greater availability or confidentiality as a component of information security. Furthermore, Ioannidis, Pym, & Williams (2011) investigated the optimal time horizon of investment in information security. Fenz & Ekelhart (2011) developed a methodology for assessment of which technology is worth to invest to, in order to increase information security, and based on it, they developed a software. Beresnevichiene, Pym, & Shiu (2010) developed a system for decision support in the field of investments in information security, based on a methodology that combines the multi-criteria value assessment and mathematical modeling.

Cavusoglu & Mishra (2004) created a model based on game theory to estimate the investment in information security. Four important aspects of successful investment in information security are identified as follows: cost estimates for the case of a security incident, investment approach using risk management, cost-effective technological configuration and values that can be obtained using more technology. Hole (2010) dealt with the assessment of the costs caused by rare events of great impact. He pointed out that difficulties in assessing the costs are results of the fact that cost depends not only on the system itself, but also on the context of the system use, such as technical requirements, the objectives of owners and users, as well as relevant regulations and laws. He noted that many similar problems may have different costs. Unlike those researches which dealt with information security of investments, Zambon (2011) developed a set of models for optimizing investment in the availability of the system: a quantitative model for decision support based on reducing the risk of unavailability, a qualitative model for risk assessment of the IT infrastructure availability, a model for support to business continuity and information system planning audits, a model for analysis and optimization of availability. Klempt, Schmidpeter, Sowa, & Tsinas (2007) presented a layered approach to business oriented information security management. The first layer represents the interface to the requirements of the business side which is collected and formulated in a way to become the requirements of information security. The second layer is done to balance the costs and benefits for each of the requirements of the first layer which enables the creation of a balanced investment strategy. The third layer is made thorough risk assessment (steps taken in the second layer can be viewed as a rough estimate) and allows automatic selection controls.

In order to determine the economic viability of costs, identification of costs arising from the unavailability of the system has to be done. Gartner's team proposed costs and consequences of downtime presented in the Figure 6 of chapter 2.

Smith grouped costs appeared due to the unavailability of the system into three groups:

- **Prevention Cost:** Cost of preventing failures;
- **Appraisal Cost:** Cost related to measurement; and
- **Failure Cost:** Costs incurred as a result of failure (Smith, 2011).

Figure 1. Costs Structure Due to the System Unavailability
Source: Scott & Malik (2001)

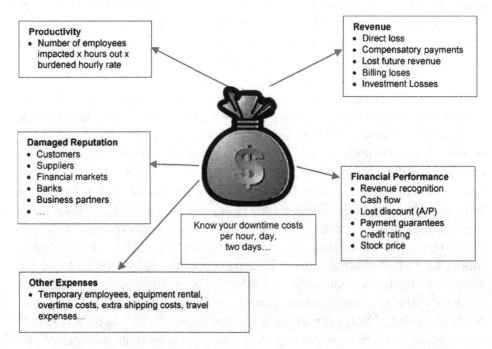

ITIL deems that cost of availability investment increase exponentially when organization aspires to the higher levels of availability which is shown in Figure 2.

OPTIMIZATION OF INVESTMENTS IN IS AVAILABILITY

Return on Investment

Calculating return on investment (ROI) is a technique that is traditionally used in decision making process related to capital budgeting. It includes comparison of return on investment in relation to the opportunity cost of capital used for investment. Deloitte surveyed 200 executives of the IT sector, 43% said they use ROI to justify the value of investments (Schniederjans et al., 2004).

Figure 2. Relationship between levels of availability and overall costs
Source: TSO report, 2007, p.63

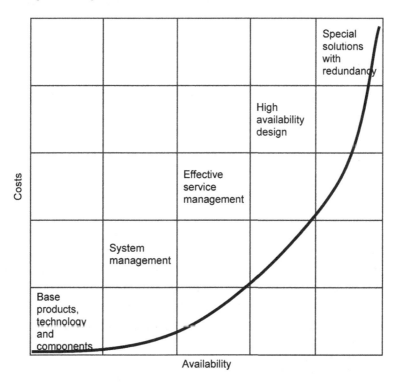

Return on investment is calculated as income from investments divided by the cost of investment. If the return on investment is greater than the opportunity cost of capital, then the investment is worth more than it costs, and should go into realization. The opportunity cost of capital can be justified by the expected return of investment in technology compared to the risk by investing in the capital market.

$$ROI = \frac{Expected\,Returns - Cost\,of\,Investment}{Cost\,of\,Investment} \tag{12}$$

ROI methodology rules for independent investment are as follows:

- If the return is greater than the opportunity cost of capital - it should be invested; and
- If the return is less than or equal to the opportunity cost of capital - it should not be invested.

The problem with this methodology is that the calculation of ROI is simple and reliable when cash flows are realized in two periods or less. When there are more than two periods, it is doubtful whether this method of calculation will give the appropriate result. In situations with more than two periods, some authors suggest a method of *"internal rate of return"*. Because of this problem, a method ROI tends to be used in addition to other methodologies (Misra, 2006).

Return on Security Investment

The concept of ROI is not directly applicable to investment in security, because these investments do not have an income, but the investment in security aimed at preventing potential loss. For this reason, the return to investment is modified into return on security investment (ROSI) in order to comply with security investments as well. ROSI evaluate potential reduction of loss due to execution of the project for which the investment needs to be done. Thus, the monetary value of the investment has to be compared with the cash value of reducing risk, which can be reached by quantitative methods.

To do a quantitative risk assessment, it is necessary to define the following terms:

- *The Single Loss Expectancy (SLE)* is the expected monetary loss in case the risk event occurs. By this approach, SLE includes total loss of one occurrence of the incident and includes all types of losses presented by Figure 6 of chapter 2.
- *The Annual Rate of Occurrence (ARO)* is probability that a certain event will occur in a single year.
- *Annual Loss Expectancy (ALE)* is a monetary loss that is expected from a specific risk for specific assets. ALE is calculated as the product of the expected loss for an event and the probability of its occurrence in a single year.

$$ALE = ARO * SLE \tag{13}$$

The methodology for ROSI calculation combines quantitative assessment of the risks and costs of implementation of security countermeasures for these risks. In other words, it compares ALE and cost of project investment which should lead to a reduction in expected losses. The formula for ROSI calculation is given below:

$$ROSI = \frac{Expected\,Loss\,Reduction - Cost\,of\,Investment}{Cost\,of\,Investment} \tag{14}$$

The implementation of effective security solutions reduces ALE: as the solution is more efficient - reduction in ALE is greater. This cash loss can be defined as the difference in expected loss with and without the implemented security solutions, i.e. the difference between the ALE and modified ALE (mALE).

$$ROSI = \frac{ALE - mALE - Cost\,of\,Invesment}{Cost\,of\,Investment} \tag{15}$$

With the introduction of the percentage of reduction formula is transformed into:

$$ROSI = \frac{ALE * Reduction\,Percentage - Cost\,of\,Invesment}{Cost\,of\,Invesment} \tag{16}$$

Disadvantages of ROSI methodology

The major disadvantage of this methodology is that calculation of ROSI is the result of many approximations. Cost of cyber security incidents and the annual rate of occurrence are difficult to assess and obtained results can vary from environment to environment. These approximations are often biased towards our perception of risk. Calculating ROSI can be easily manipulated in the absence of relevant data and serve the interests of users to justify investment decisions rather than to facilitate decision-making by providing relevant data. It is therefore necessary to ensure the accuracy of statistical data used in calculating the ROSI. However, adequate information security incidents are difficult to find since companies are reluctant to provide information about their security incidents.

Cost/Benefit Analysis

Cost/benefit analysis involves the estimation of the net benefits associated with alternative courses of action. This technique entails comparing the present value of investments and benefits associated with the investments. Cost/benefit analysis is a widely used tool for decision-making in public and private organizations and is used for a wide variety of problems, including making decisions on IT investments. Cost/benefit analysis involves identifying costs and benefits of each alternative investment, discounting of costs and benefits to the present value, and choosing the best alternatives according to predetermined criteria. Cost/benefit analysis can be used to assess the independent investment and select one or more among a set of independent and dependent investments. Like most analysis, cost/benefit analysis consists of a series of steps or degrees. Figure 3 shows the five common stages in the implementation of cost/benefit analysis. These different stages include: define problem; identify costs and benefits; quantify costs and benefits; compare alternatives; and perform sensibility analysis (Schniederjans et al., 2004).

The following formula is an example of calculating the current value of the investment in security measures (Faisst, Prokein, & Wegman, 2007; Brecht & Nowey, 2012):

$$NPV = -I_0 + \sum_{t=1}^{T} \frac{\Delta E\left(L_t\right) + \Delta OCC_t - C_t}{\left(1 + i_r\right)^t} \tag{17}$$

Figure 3. The Five Stages of Cost/Benefit Analysis
Source: Schniederjans et al. (2004), p. 145

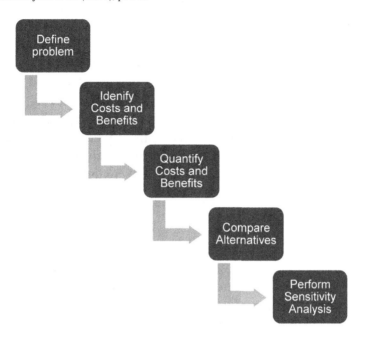

I_0- initial investment for security measure

$\Delta E\left(L_t\right)$- reduction of expected loss in t

ΔOCC_t – reduction of opportunity costs in t

C_t - cost of security measure in t

i_r – discount rate

Analytic Hierarchy Process (AHP)

AHP is a systematic approach, developed in the 1980s, with a goal to introduce structure and well-defined methodology based on sound mathematical principles into the decision-making process based on experience, intuition and heuristics. This approach helps analyze the problem including both quantitative and qualitative criteria. It provides a formalized approach in which the economic justification of time invested in the decision-making process provides better quality solutions to complex problems (Bhushan & Rai, 2004). Originally developed as a technique of decision making, AHP is applied to a wide range of major projects and problems in the decision-making process. A special application of AHP is found in making IT investment decisions. Analytic hierarchy process uses the comparison of alternatives in pairs to establish the weighting factors for model-making, setting priorities among alternatives and generate accurate statistics to confirm the decision. AHP is a complete decision-making process that allows a good understanding of more factors or more conditions in the decision-making process. An additional advantage of this methodology is that it requires all of the factors in the decision making environment to be directly compared with all other factors, providing a more inclusive consideration of the interaction and value of each factor relative to all the other factors (Schniederjans et al., 2004).

The AHP Procedure

AHP provides tools for the problem decomposition in the hierarchy of the sub-problems that are easier to understand and objectively evaluated. Subjective assessments are converted into numerical values and are processed in a manner to enable the ranking of each of the alternatives on a numerical scale. AHP procedure comprises of six steps:

Step 1 - Establish the Decision Hierarchy: The problem is broken down into a hierarchy of objectives, criteria, sub-criteria and alternatives. The hierarchy shows the relationship between the elements of one level with elements of the lower level. Problem to be studied and analyzed is at the root of the hierarchy. The leaves are the alternatives to be compared. There are different criteria and sub-criteria between these two levels. It is important to note that when comparing elements at each level, decision-maker only compares the contribution of lower-level elements to the elements at the upper level.

Step 2 - Establish the Pair-Wise Comparison of Alternatives: Data about qualitative relationships for each pair of alternatives, correspondingly hierarchical structure are collected from experts and decision-makers. Experts can evaluate elements and declare them as equal or give priority to one over the other (equally preferred, moderately preferred, strongly preferred, etc). Comparisons are made for each criterion and then conversion from qualitative to quantitative form.

Step 3 - Compute the Factor Priorities: Decision-maker uses the previously determined comparison ratings to compute a set of priorities for the factors. Process begins with conversion of complete comparison ratings in the tables for each factor from step 2 into decimal form. The greater the number of places behind the decimal point, the greater the precision of the resulting values.

Step 4 - Compute the Factor Weight Priorities: Decision-maker uses the same approach as that from step 2 and 3 and applies it to comparison of the factors with other factors.

Step 5 - Compute the Overall Decision Priorities: Decision-maker uses the factor weights from step 4 and the values from step 3 to compute expected values for the overall decision.

Step 6 - Determine Consistency Ratios: First, consistency index should be calculated because comparisons made by this method are subjective and AHP tolerates inconsistency which compensates elements of redundancy in the approach. If consistency index reaches the required level, then answer the comparisons have to be re-examined. Formula for consistency index (C) is:

$$CI = (\lambda max - n) / (n - 1) \tag{18}$$

where CI is the consistency index value, n is the number of items being compared and λ is the average of the weighted sum vector values. A generic hierarchical network is shown in Figure 4.

Figure 4. A Generic Hierarchical Network

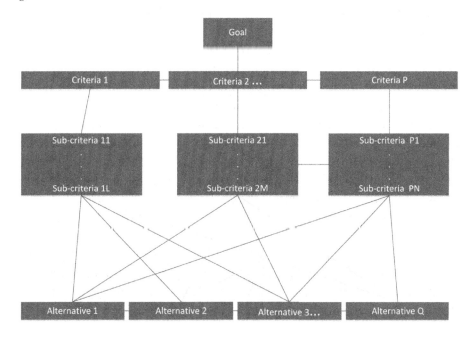

Disadvantages of AHP

Despite the widespread use of the AHP in different areas and at different levels of the hierarchy of decision making, AHP has criticized on several grounds. The first problem is that the possible rank reversal. In many scenarios, the ranking between two existing alternatives obtained by the AHP may change if a new alternative is added. Following issues related to the AHP are noted in literature:

- Vendors get improperly penalized.
- The ratio scale is inaccurate.
- The process may generate inconsistencies as an artefact of its calculation that have nothing to do with consistency of judgment.
- Rank reversal (Bhushan & Rai, 2004).

Game Theory

Game theory (GT) is an extension of the theory of decision-making. As with the problems of decision-making theory, GT problems have multiple strategies or choices between alternatives. One of the differences between DT and GT is that GT problem exists in conflict type of decision environment. In conflict situations, there is more than one person making the choice. Like chess, when one player plays a move, the other player responds to the retracted move. This game moves and counter-moves continues until the end of the game. There are many situations in which IT is very important to understanding and responding to competitive moves or behavior. As such, the GT is an important methodology for evaluating IT investments (Schniederjans et al., 2004). In the GT problem, the optimal solution is possible if both players play the perfect game that leads to victory.

Cavusoglu & Mishra (2004) argue that the traditional approach to decision theory for evaluating investment in IT security is not adequate, because although intuitive, it treats security technology as a black box and does not take into account that the context of IT security is different from the others general IT investments. They argue that in the context of investment in safety, the organization struggles with strategic adversaries who are looking for potential vulnerabilities in the information system. Therefore, IT security can be treated as a kind of game between the organization and the header. Game theory is used to analyze the problem in which players gain depends on the interaction between the strategies of players. The issue of investment in safety is that turnover generated from security investments depends on the degree of security threats. Investments in safety do not help only to prevent security breaches through reduction of the vulnerabilities that attackers can exploit, but also as a discourage attackers. Based on the above ideas, Cavusoglu & Mishra (2004) used an approach based on game theory to determine optimal investment level in IT security.

Real Options Analysis

Real options analysis was first developed as a technique for decision support in the area of capital investments. The term *real* is related to adaptation of mathematical models which are used to assess the financial options for use in more tangible investments. The option gives the holder the right but not the obligation to take ownership of the property on which the option is based in the future. If future event removes or otherwise reduces sources of uncertainty at a satisfactory level, organization can take advantage of its possibilities and continue to implement the full extent. If, however, the uncertainty continues or is not resolved in a satisfactory manner, the period of validity of the option may be extended or the option can easily expire, thus limiting downside exposure to future losses. This approach reconciles financial and strategic point of view in the decision-making process that are made in an environment with uncertain parameters - specifically for the evaluation of flexibility. The core of the analysis of real options for investments in IT assets consists of:

- Identification and assessment of the possibilities of the components in the project; and
- The selection and application of mathematical models to value financial option that serves to quantify the current value in the selection of components that will be performed later.

The real options theory is applied in several areas of information systems and research in the field of software engineering, for example, re-use software components and stability of the software architecture (Bahsoon, 2005). It have been made attempts to use the real options analysis for explaining or guiding investment decisions in the field of information security. Gordon, Loeb, & Lucyshyn (2003) have explained why it seems that much of the security expenditures made after "waiting to see what will happen" even though expenses to prevent vulnerabilities that violate security information is rapidly growing in recent years. They claim that one of the key drivers of current investment in information security is frequent occurrence of recorded events that impair safety. Further, they noted that it is reactive as opposed to proactive approach according to which a considerable part of the investment in information security is in accordance with the applied real options approach to capital investment. Daneva (2006) have proposed a framework for making decisions about investments in security which is based on a real options model and he argued that this approach allows flexibility in the decision-making process. Harris, Herron, & Iwanicki (2008) have explained the real options analysis as a procedure that is used to modify the ROI calculation, taking into account the value that the current project can contribute to future projects. This approach usually increases ROI of projects such as investments in IT infrastructure, where the cost of implementation of a whole new infrastructure for a single project or for the needs of a business unit are so enormous that no department or function could ever justify the start of investment in new infrastructure. However, the overall business value of new infrastructure if it will be used in all business units in the organization can be huge. Real options analysis provides a technique to justify the first project based on the future value derived.

Value at Security Risk (VaR)

VaR calculates maximum potential loss due to security breaches during the reporting period with the given confidence level. More formally, VaR describes percentile of the predicted loss distribution in a given period. After getting quantification of risk, the choice of optimal security portfolio should be done using cost/benefit analysis. Ozcelik & Rees (2005) recommend following steps for the VaR analysis:

1. **Identification of Threats:** The first phase of the risk assessment is to identify potential threats or risks for organization, such as malicious attacks, denial of service, unauthorized access to private information, delete or modify sensitive information, viruses, worms, attempting to learn passwords, hacking, fraud, natural disasters, sabotage and user errors. Each organization may be at risk for some or all of these types of potential risks.

2. **Assessment of the Probability of Threats:** Assessing the probability of threats can be obtained compared to external databases containing historical data on security incidents which are commercially available. Another way of assessing the probability is based on internal database of historical data which may not be as large or through expert assessments. Based on these three sources it is possible to estimate the probability distribution of threats with which the company can face. Possible sce-

narios of risk for the organization can then be carried out based on the probability distribution of individual risk.

3. **VaR Assessment:** After identification of various risks and their estimated probabilities presented through the distribution of probability of risk as well as identification of possible risk scenarios, the next step is to calculate the VaR. In order to achieve this, it is first necessary to calculate the variability of risk factors based on the estimated distribution of different risk scenarios. It should calculate the loss for the worst case scenario for all cases in the scenario in a specified time horizon. This is basis for estimation of probability distribution of loss in the worst case. For this assessment can be used techniques of approximation of probability distribution (Monte Carlo), or some derivative assumptions of normality, symmetry and asymmetry of distribution. The last step involves using the estimated probability distribution of loss in the worst case and determine VaR identifying points on the curve distribution, which covers 95% of the area under the curve.

Wang, Chaudhury, & Rao (2008) have applied this method to measure daily losses with which the organization is facing as a result of information security risk, and used extreme value analysis to quantify VaR. Hulten (2009) pointed out that companies already have tools, methods and measurements to express the levels of risk and their economic consequences, referring to the Value-at-Risk and Value-at-Risk type metrics. He stressed out possibility of transformation of entities and metrics used in the field of information

Figure 5. VaR Curve

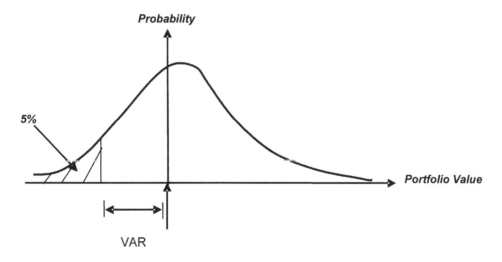

security to the Value-at-Risk entities and metrics. This enables managers to understand, compare and assess information security risks and their economic consequences with the risks generated by other sources, strategy or investment decisions. In this way, management is provided with the firmer and more rational basis for decision-making on investment in information security. Dealing with risks in the field of information security with low frequency but high consequences, Hinz & Malinowski (2006) also recommended the use of the theory of extreme values and the calculation of VaR.

REAL WORLD CASES

Risk IT Case Study: Risk IT Framework for IT Risk Management: A Case Study of National Stock Exchange of India Limited

National Stock Exchange (NSE) is the largest stock exchange in India catering to 1,200-plus members. Globally, NSE has been ranked second in stock index options and third in single stock futures and stock index futures. The business processes of NSE are heavily dependent on IT. Average daily turnover of trades processed by NSE are INR 1,441,010. At a national level, NSE is a critical organization for the Indian economy and is identified as one of its most sensitive organizations. The criticality of business operations required NSE to focus on risk management as an integral element of its day-to-day business processes. Up until this new focus, the existing risk management process mainly focused on addressing business risk. The IT risk assessment method was complementary to the business risk processes, and the approach adopted was periodic assessment (once a year), which until now was considered adequate. However, during the review of risk assessment, it was observed that the dynamic nature of the business environment had been prompting frequent changes in IT infrastructure. These changes constituted not only changes in hardware, but also included revamping applications and identifying new service delivery channels. This prompted the decision to revisit the IT risk management approach. Available at: http://www.isaca.org/Knowledge-Center/cobit/Pages/Risk-IT-Case-Study-Risk-IT-Framework-for-IT-Risk-Management-A-Case-Study-of-National-Stock-Exchange-of-India-Limited.aspx (Accessed on 2016-12-28)

CHAPTER SUMMARY

The main objective of this chapter was to provide brief overview of the models regarding economic viability of investments in IS availability. Seven methods for optimization of IT investments are presented: return on investment, return on security investment, cost/benefit analysis, analytic hierarchy process, game theory, real options analysis, value at security risk. In summary:

Return on investment technique includes comparison of return on investment in relation to the opportunity cost of capital used for investment. Return on security investment (ROSI) means comparison of the monetary value of the investment with the cash value of reducing risk. This technique entails comparing the present value of investments and benefits associated with the investments. Cost/benefit analysis involves identifying costs and benefits of each alternative investment, discounting of costs and benefits to the present value, and choosing the best alternatives according to predetermined criteria. Analytic hierarchy process uses the comparison of alternatives in pairs to establish the weighting factors for model-making, setting priorities among alternatives and generate accurate statistics to confirm the decision. Game theory is an extension of the theory of decision-making. As with the problems of decision-making theory, GT problems have multiple strategies or choices between alternatives. Real options analysis for investments in IT assets consists of: identification and assessment of the possibilities of the components in the project; and selection and application of mathematical models to value financial option that serves to quantify the current value in the selection of components that will be performed later. VaR calculates maximum potential loss due to security breaches during the reporting period with the given confidence level.

REFERENCES

Ahmad, F., & Arshad, N. H. (2014). Value Delivery of Information Technology Investment: A Conceptual Framework. *International Journal of Computer Theory and Engineering*, *6*(2), 150–154. doi:10.7763/IJCTE.2014.V6.854

Anderson, R. (2001). Why information security is hard-an economic perspective. *Proceedings of theSecurity Applications Conference*. doi:10.1109/ACSAC.2001.991552

Anderson, R., & Moore, T. (2006). The Economics of Information Security: A Survey and Open Questions. *Science*, *314*(610-613), 1–27.

Bahsoon, R. K. (2005). *Evaluating Architectural Stability with Real Options Theory*. University of London.

Bardhan, I., & Sougstad, R. (2004). Prioritizing a portfolio of information technology investment projects. *Journal of Management Information Systems, 21*(2), 33–60.

Beresnevichiene, Y., Pym, D., & Shiu, S. (2010). Decision support for systems security investment. *Proceedings of the2010 IEEE/IFIP Network Operations and Management Symposium Workshops* (pp. 118–125). doi:10.1109/NOMSW.2010.5486590

Bhushan, N., & Rai, K. (2004). *Strategic Decision Making Applying the Analytic Hierarchy Process*. Springer-Verlag.

Bodin, L. D., Gordon, L. A., & Loeb, M. P. (2005). Evaluating Information Security Investments Using the Analytic Hierarchy Process. *Communications of the ACM, 48*(2), 79–83. doi:10.1145/1042091.1042094

Brecht, M., & Nowey, T. (2013). A closer look at information security costs. In *The Economics of Information Security and Privacy* (pp. 3–24). Springer Berlin Heidelberg. doi:10.1007/978-3-642-39498-0_1

Cavusoglu, H., Mishra, B., & Raghunathan, S. (2004). A model for evaluating IT security investments. *Communications of the ACM, 47*(7), 87–92. doi:10.1145/1005817.1005828

Daneva, M. (2006). *Applying real options thinking to information security in networked organizations (No. TR-CTI)*. Centre for Telematics and Information Technology, University of Twente.

Fenz, S., & Ekelhart, A. (2011). Information Security Risk Management: In which security solutions is it worth investing? *Communications of the Association for Information Systems, 28*(1), 329–356.

Gordon, L. A., & Loeb, M. P. (2002). The economics of information security investment. *ACM Transactions on Information and System Security, 5*(4), 438–457. doi:10.1145/581271.581274

Gordon, L. A., & Loeb, M. P. (2006). Budgeting process for information security expenditures. *Communications of the ACM, 49*(1), 121–126. doi:10.1145/1107458.1107465

Gordon, L. A., Loeb, M. P., & Lucyshyn, W. (2003). *Information security expenditures and real options: A wait-and-see approach*. Computer Security Journal.

Hamaker, J. L. (2009). *Information Technology Investment Methodologies: an Investigation Into Method/Technology Fit.* University of Nebraska.

Harris, M. D. S., Herron, D., & Iwanicki, S. (2008). *The business value of IT: Managing risks, optimizing performance, and measuring results.* CRC Press. doi:10.1201/9781420064759

Hinz, D. J., & Malinowski, J. (2006, January). Assessing the Risks of IT Infrastructure—A Personal Network Perspective. *Proceedings of the 39th Annual Hawaii International Conference on System SciencesHICSS'06 (Vol. 8,* pp. 172a-172a). IEEE.

Hole, K., & Netland, L. H. (2010). Toward risk assessment of large-impact and rare events. *IEEE Security and Privacy, 8*(3), 21–27. doi:10.1109/MSP.2010.55

Hulthén, R. (2009). Communicating the economic value of security investments: value at security risk. In Managing Information Risk and the Economics of Security (pp. 121-140). Springer US. doi:10.1007/978-0-387-09762-6_6

Ioannidis, C., & Pym, D. (2009). *Investments and trade-offs in the economics of information security.* Cryptography and Data Security. doi:10.1007/978-3-642-03549-4_9

Ioannidis, C., Pym, D., & Williams, J. (2011, June). Fixed costs, investment rigidities, and risk aversion in information security: A utility-theoretic approach.*Proceedings of the Tenth Workshop on the Economics of Information Security (WEIS).*

Klempt, P., Schmidpeter, H., Sowa, S., & Tsinas, L. (2007, November). Business Oriented Information Security Management–A Layered Approach. *Proceedings of the OTM Confederated International Conferences "On the Move to Meaningful Internet Systems"* (pp. 1835-1852). Springer Berlin Heidelberg. doi:10.1007/978-3-540-76843-2_49

Kumar, R. L. (2004). A framework for assessing the business value of information technology infrastructures. *Journal of Management Information Systems,* (2): 11–32.

Misra, R. B. (2006). Evolution of the Philosophy of Investments in IT Projects. *Issues in Informing Science and Information Technology, 3.*

Ozcelik, Y., & Rees, J. (2005). A New Approach for Information Security Risk Assessment: Value at Risk.

Schniederjans, M. J., Hamaker, J. L., & Schniederjans, A. M. (2004). *Information Technology Investment Decision - Making Methodology*. World Scientific Publishing Co. Pte. Ltd.

Scott, D., & Malik, W. (2001). Best Practices in Business Continuity Planning. *Proceedings of theSymposium/ITxpo*.

Serafeimidis, V. (1997). *Interpreting the evaluation of information systems investments: conceptual and operational explorations* [Doctoral dissertation]. University of London.

Smith, D. J. (2011). *Reliability, Maintainability and Risk* (8th ed.). Elsevier LTD.

Von Faisst, U., Prokein, O., & Wegmann, N. (2007). Ein Modell zur dynamischen Investitionsrechnung von IT-Sicherheitsmaßnahmen. *Zeitschrift für Betriebswirtschaft*, *77*(5), 511–538. doi:10.1007/s11573-007-0039-y

Wang, J., Chaudhury, A., & Rao, H. R. (2008). Research Note — A Value-at-Risk Approach to Information Security Investment. *Information Systems Research*, *19*(1), 106–120. doi:10.1287/isre.1070.0143

Zambon, E. (2011). *Towards Optimal IT Availability Planning: Methods and Tools*. University of Twente. doi:10.3990/1.9789036531023

Chapter 4
Bayesian Belief Networks in IT Investment Decision Making

ABSTRACT

This section aims at describing the concept of Bayesian Belief Networks (BBN), building principles and application of BBN and influence diagrams, as well as the reasons why BBN are considered an adequate tool for IS availability modeling.

BAYESIAN BELIEF NETWORKS (BBN)

The main reason for choosing this instrument is its applicability in the treatment of problems of this domain. While writing about the application of BBN on modeling operational risk information technology in financial institutions Neil, Marquez, & Fenton (2008) argued that the main advantages of BBN are in enabling a combination of statistical and qualitative data and mapping the causal structure of the process, thus making it easier to understand and communicate with business users. BBN method enables combining proactive loss indicators with reactive consequence measurement, considering experts' judgments using a qualitative risk assessment, working with incomplete data and still get a reasonable prediction. Besides that, by using BBN one can implement strong scenario analysis, test the robustness of the results, have a tool for visual reasoning and help in documentation, conduct a comparative analysis of alternative scenarios and check the robustness of the IT infrastructure on the changes in the design.

DOI: 10.4018/978-1-5225-2268-3.ch004

Figure 1. BBN example

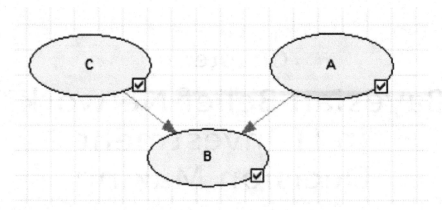

BBN are graphical models that combine the graph and probability theory. Each BBN consists of two elements: directed acyclic graphs representing the structure, and a set of conditional probability tables -CPT. The nodes in the structure correspond to the variables of interest, and the edges are interpreted in terms of conditional probabilities according to Bayes theorem. For many practical applications, an edge represents a direct causal effect.

BBN must contain CPT for each variable which quantifies a relationship between the variable and its "parent" in the graph (Darwiche, 2010). Bayesian network can be used to answer probabilistic questions about the variables and their relationships represented by the network. For example, a network can be used to find out, by using Bayes theorem, an updated knowledge of the state of a variables subset when other variables (the evidence variables) are observed. This process of computing the posterior distribution of variables given evidence is called probabilistic inference. A Bayesian network can thus

Figure 2. CPT example

Node properties: B

| General | Definition | Observation Cost | Format | Documentation | User properties | Value |

Add   Insert   ✗

C		State0			State1	
A		State0	State1		State0	State1
State0		0.7	0.6		0.4	0.2
State1		0.3	0.4		0.6	0.8

be considered a mechanism for automatically applying Bayes' theorem to complex problems (Ding, 2010). For two events, Bayes' theorem is represented as follows:

$$P(A \mid B) = \frac{P(B \mid A)P(A)}{P(B)} \tag{19}$$

This formula means that it is possible to calculate the conditional probability of event A, for a given event B, using conditional probabilities of event B, for a given event A and unconditional probabilities of event A and event B. In the case that states of any nodes are fixed, Bayes' theorem can be used for propagation in backward direction, and the thus calculate posterior probabilities for every node in the graph. This is the basic scenario in BBN analysis (Carol, 2003). BBN can be used in three ways:

- **Causation Reasoning:** Calculation of probabilities that consequence is caused by the occurrence of the particular event (probability that cancer is caused by smoking).
- **Diagnostic Reasoning:** Search probability that the consequence will happen if a particular event occurs, (probability that someone will get cancer if he smokes).
- **Support Reasoning:** Search the interaction among the causes (Yu, Zheng, & Qian, 2009).

Bayesian network is a directed acyclic graph (DAG), which defines the factorization of the joint probability distribution of variables represented by graph nodes. The factorization determines directional relationships in the graph. More precisely, in the DAG, G = (V, E), V denotes the set of nodes and E set of directed links between pairs of nodes. The joint probability distribution P (X_V), for the set of (usually discrete) variables Xv indexed by V, can be factorized as $P(X_v) = \prod_{v \in V} P(X_v \mid X_{pa(v)})$ where $X_{pa(v)}$) denotes "parents" of node Xv. During construction of Bayesian networks, it is advisable to keep the number of parent nodes per one child node to a minimum. Factorization in the previous equation expresses a set of assumptions about independence, which are presented in the graph in such a way that direct links exist only between interdependent nodes. The combination of the assumption of independence and a small set of parents for each node, enables the conditional probability calculation and efficient inference in Bayesian networks.

Any conditional probabilities distribution $P(X_v | X_{pa(v)})$ is a set of rules, where each rule (conditional probability) has the form:

If the $X_{pa(v)} = x_{pa(v)}$ than $X_v = x_v$ with probability z

where x_v represents the values associated with X_v and, $x_{pa(v)}$ vector with values associated with parents of node X_v. For example, if the node X can take one of five values, and if this variable has four parents of which may have three values, then the $P(X_v | X_{pa(v)})$ is a set of $5 * 3^4 = 405$ rules in the form shown above. Presented notation, using the rules, only implicitly appears in Bayesian networks. Instead there is explicit notation, where each of the conditional probability $P(X_v | X_{pa(v)})$ is presented as $P(X_v = x_v | X_{pa(v)} = x_{pa(v)})$ = z or even simpler $P(x_v | x_{pa(v)}) = z$ (Kjaerulff & Madsen, 2008).

Random variables are presented as nodes, and uncertainty is expressed over the probability density. The probability density expresses modeler's belief that a random variable can take different values, depending on the status of parent nodes on the incoming edges. The nodes and associated variables can be classified into three groups:

- **Target Node:** The node for which valuation a network is constructed. A typical example of such a node is "system available."
- **Intermediate Nodes:** Nodes that have limited information, or just a "belief." Associated variables are hidden variables. Typically hidden variables are of qualitative dimension, such as "quality of development", "the reputation of the manufacturer", or "quality at a certain phase of development," without discussing "quality" in detail.
- **Visible (Informative) Nodes:** Nodes that represent variables whose values are observable. Some examples are the nodes that are visible features of the system for monitoring "There is no failure during testing" and "all quality requirements are met" (Gran, 2002).

The definition of Bayesian networks and conditional probability factorization require compliance with the assumption of independence. Two events are independent if the occurrence of the first event does not change the probability of the second event. In the probability theory, two events A and B are independent if $P(A \cap B) = P(A) P(B)$. In other words, the probability of occurrence of both events is equal to the product of the probability of occurrence of each event. In graph theory, the word independent usually means disjunction between variables or denotes a pair of variables that are not next-door neighbors. In this context, independence is a form of not being a direct neighborhood. Independent set is a collection of nodes where there is no pair or where nodes are direct neighbors. One way to check the independence among the variables is known as d-separation (Pearl, 1988).

The d-separation is based on three basic types of connections in Bayesian network:

Serial connections X> Y> Z: Data can be transferred via the connection until it is not known the state of node Y. Figure 3 shows an example of a serial connection. In case it is known whether the server is running (unknown state variable Y), information on whether the air conditioner is operating (variable X) gives new information. This update may affect the probability of system availability (variable Z), i.e. If the air-condition in the server room works properly, the greater the probability that the system is available. On the other hand, if it is known that the server does not work (state of Y is known), then information about the state of the air-condition does not affect the probability of system availability.

The diverging relationship, X <Y-> Z, presented on the Figure 4: Information can be transferred via the connection until the state of node Y is not known. Example: If point of interest is the dependence on external service supplier (variable Y), and it is found that service is not dependent on external supplier, then additional knowledge about the variable "external supplier does not deliver adequate service" will not bring any more information about the variable "suboptimal requirements management " (Z) than information acquired by monitoring the variable "service depends on external supplier" only. On the other hand, if it is not known whether the service depends on the external supplier, the observation that the organization implemented a sub-optimal requirements management, increases the belief that an external supplier does not deliver adequate service.

Converged connections X> Y <Z: Data can be transferred via the connection only if information about the state of Y or one of its descendants is available. For example, if it is not known that the "system is unavailable" (Y) and that "external supplier does not deliver adequate service" (X), then

Figure 3. Serial connection in Bayesian networks

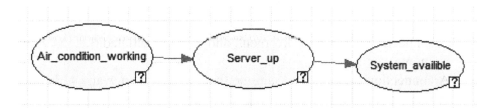

Figure 4. The diverging and converging connection in Bayesian networks
adapted from (Fineman, 2010)

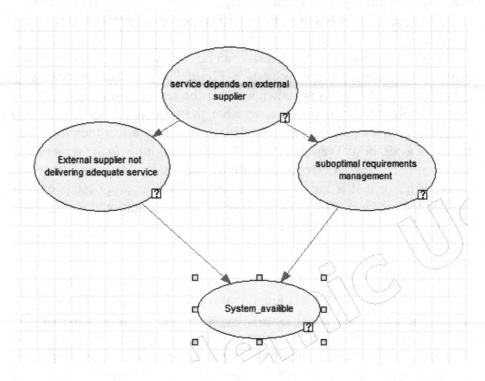

it will affect belief that the organization using a "sub-optimal requirements management" (Z). In addition, information that "the system is not available" leads to the following conclusion: it is more likely that the unavailability is caused by the "external supplier does not deliver adequate service" rather than "sub-optimal management requirements." On the other hand, if there is not information about the state of system availability, information of the quality of a requirements management process will not affect the belief about whether the external supplier delivers the appropriate service or not.

Two variables X and Z are d-separated if for all paths between X and Z there is intermediate node, and at least one of the following requirements is fulfilled:

- A connection is serial or divergent, and Y is instantiated (i.e., its value is known), or
- A connection is converged, and neither state of Y, nor any of his descendants is not known.

In the example presented in Figure 4, a set of nodes {external supplier does not deliver adequate service, sub-optimal management requirements} is d-separated by nodes {service depends on an external supplier} and {system available}, because {external supplier does not deliver adequate service} blocks path (dependent on service the external supplier, external supplier does not deliver adequate service, the system is available) and {suboptimal requirements management} blocks paths (service depends on an external supplier, sub-optimal requirements management, the system is available). In both cases, the node that blocks connection is on the path. Furthermore, {service depends on an external supplier} separates {external supplier does not deliver adequate service} and {suboptimal management requirements}, where {service depends on an external supplier} diverges on the only path between them, {an external supplier does not deliver adequate, service depends on the external supplier, sub-optimal management requirements}.

If X and Z are not d-separated, then they are d-connected. Dependence and independence relation between nodes can change based on what is known (and not known). In other words, the available evidence plays a significant role in determining the dependence and independence relationships. One can distinguish different patterns of causality supported by Bayesian networks: predictive, diagnostic, explaining away.

These patterns can be explained by using an example (Figure 5). It will be assumed that all nodes are discrete and have only two states: "true" and "false", to make an example easier for understanding.

- **Predictive:** If it is believed that there was a "growth in dollar exchange rate," then the probability that the investment budget will be meager, increased.
- **Diagnostic:** If it is found that the investment budget is not sufficient then increases the likelihood that growth in dollar exchange rate occurred and suboptimal procurement management.
- **Explaining Away:** If it is found that the investment budget is not sufficient, then it is most likely explanation "Growth dollar exchange rate", and revised the probability of "optimal procurement management" is still low. However, if it is also found that the system is not available, then it can be concluded that is "insufficient budget for investments" likely caused by non-optimal procurement management, rather than increase the dollar. So "insufficient budget for investment" is clarified by the observation that the "system unavailable" with whom there is no direct connection ("away") (Fineman, 2010).

Figure 5. Example of reasoning using Bayesian networks

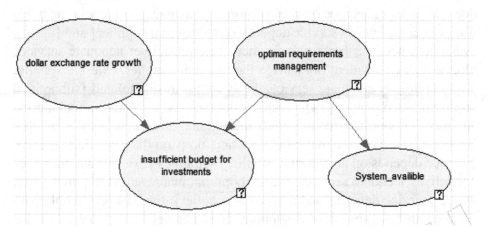

The process of applying BBN method consists of three phases: a) construction of the network topology, b) filling the conditional probability tables and c) solving the network (Gran, 2002).

Construction of Bayesian Networks

As noted above, Bayesian networks can be described using the DAG as a qualitative component and the joint probability distribution as a quantitative part. This distribution factorizes into the collection of conditional probability distributions depending on DAG's structure.

Construction of Bayesian networks has two phases. First, with respect to the modeled problem, it is necessary to identify the relevant variables and (causal) relations among them. The resulting DAG implies a set of assumptions about the dependence and independence among the variables that are implemented through the joint probability distribution. The second phase is specifying sets of conditional probability distributions, $P(X_v | X_{pa(v)})$, one for each family {V} presented in DAG.

Bayesian networks can be built: manually, (semi-) automatically from data, or using a combination of manual and process-driven data. If combination method is used then partial information on the structure and parameters (i.e., conditional probabilities) are combined with statistical data obtained from the database of cases (i.e., the previous observation values of the variables). Manual building Bayesian networks can be a task that requires hard work, great skills and creativity, as well as direct communication with experts in the field of the modeled problem. Once built (either manually or automatically), the Bayesian network parameters can be continuously updated with new information which comes to light. Therefore, the model can initially roughly guess parameters' values, and will gradually improve, as new information becomes available.

As an example, the problem concerning the unavailability of e-banking servers it is considered. To keep the model simple, only two possible causes, will be analyzed: hardware failure and error (crash) in the operating system. It will be assumed that the only observation, except knowing that the server is not available, is information about patching operating system. If it is known that the operating system was updated last night, then it is assumed that the probable cause of the unavailability is an error in the operating system, not a hardware failure. To solve the problem using Bayesian network, the variables and their possible states must be identified first.

The variables and their possible states are presented in the Table 1. The next illustration shows the structure of the Bayesian network for this problem.

The Figure 6 indicates that the variable "Hardware_failure" and "OS_error" have a causal link to the variable "Server_available", which is in this case the target variable. Also, the variable "OS_error" has a causal link to the variable "Update_last_night". The second step is to specify a conditional probability table (CPT) for each variable. If there are not any information about the states of other variables, it can be expected that a bug in the software happens once in a hundred cases. Then, according to Table 2, the probability distribution for the variable OS_error can be specified as:

P (OS_error) = (0.01,0.99)

Similarly, it can be assumed that a hardware failure occurs once in 1,000 cases and therefore specify:

P (Hardware_failure) = (0.001,0.999)

Table 1. Variables and states for the server availability example

Variable	Domain
Server_availible	{yes, no}
Hardware_failure	{yes, no}
OS_error	{yes, no}
Update_last_night	{updated, not_updated}

Figure 6. Bayesian network for the server availability problem

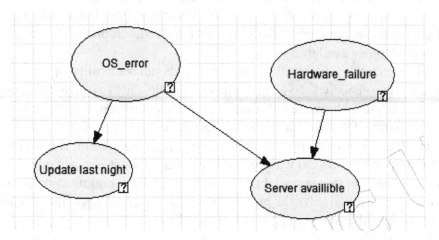

For the variable "Update_last_night" it is necessary to specify two conditional probability distributions, one for each value of the variable "OS_error". For the variable "Server_available" it is necessary to specify four distribution conditional probabilities, one for each combination of state variables of its parents, "OS_error" and "Hardware_failure". Conditional probabilities for the two variables are given in Table 2 and 3, respectively.

Table 2. CPT for the node Update_last_night P(Update_last_night| OS_error)

Update_last_night	OS_error	
	Yes	No
Updated	0.9	0.05
Not_updated	0.1	0.95

Table 3. CPT table for the variable server_availible P(Server_available| OS_error, Hardware_failure)

Server_Availible	OS_Error	Hardware_Failure
0	Yes	Yes
0	No	Yes
0.2	Yes	No
0.9999	No	No

Table 3 shows that even though operating system error occured, there is a possibility that the server is available despite the fact that not every operating system error causes the unavailability of the server. Also, the table shows that although there are no errors on operating system, and hardware is working properly, again there is a possibility that the server is unavailable. That can be explained by the fact that all the variables affecting server availability are not included in the model. This model can be solved by using Genie 2.0, a software tool for Bayesian networks modeling. The following conclusions can be drawn:

- The probability that the server will be available P (Server_availible) = 99.87%.
- The probability that the server unavailability was caused by a hardware failure P (Hardware_failure = Yes | Server_available = No) = 76.22%.
- The probability that the unavailability caused by software error P (OS_error = Yes | Server_available = No) = 16.25%.

If there is information that administrators updated the server operating system last night, then the probability that the unavailability is caused by an error in the operating system increases significantly P(OS_error = Yes | Server_availible = No, Update_last_night = Updated)=97.05%. Probability that the unavailability is caused by hardware failure has been reduced to P(Hardware_failure = Yes | Server_available = No, Update_last_night = date) = 3.14%.

Noicy OR

Although Bayesian networks significantly reduce the number of parameters needed to specify the joint probability distribution, the number of parameters in the model remains one of the major bottlenecks of this framework. This problem especially occurs when the model contains nodes with multiple parents. For every node which has a parent node, the conditional probability table (CPT) has to be fulfilled. CPT contains a set of discrete probability distributions organized that include all possible combinations of the parents' states. For example, if all variables in the model have binary values and variable X has three parents, CPT corresponding X will have $2^3 = 8$ probability distribution (as there are 3 X parents, each with two states). Therefore, the number of parameters in the CPT grows exponentially with the number of parent nodes and easily achieves value, which is not acceptable for a real life application. One way to reduce this number is to assume a functional relationship that defines the interaction between all the parents of a node. The most widely accepted and applied solutions for this problem is the Noisy-OR model (Pearl, 1988). Noisy-OR model gives a causal interpretation of the interaction between the parent and child nodes and assumes that all causes (parents) are independent of each other regarding their ability to influence the effect variable (child). Given these assumptions Noisy-OR model provides a logarithmic reduction in the number of parameters needed for the CPT construction, which practically makes building large models for real life problems feasible. Noisy-OR gates belong to a family „independence of causal influences" (ICI) models. Name of the family reflects the underlying assumption behind these models, which states that the impact of each modeled cause to the effect is independent of other causes. The word "noisy" in the name indicates that the causal interaction is not deterministic, in the sense that every cause can produce the effect with a certain probability. The second part of the name - OR (or) is derived from the functional relationship, which determines the way in which the independent causes combine to produce a common effect.

Noisy - OR model can be represented as a probabilistic extension of deterministic OR models. In a similar manner as the deterministic OR model, Noisy-OR model assumes that the presence of any of the causes X_i is sufficient to obtain the presence of effect Y, and X_i ability to produce the effect is independent of the presence of other causes. However, the presence of causes X in Noisy-OR model does not guarantee that effect Y will happen. For modeling Noisy-OR using a logic of deterministic OR model, the concept of an inhibitor node is introduced. It reflects probabilistic relationships between each cause and effect variable. The general model is shown in Figure 5. Independence of the causes is presented by introducing inhibitor nodes Yi, whose conditional probabilities table (CPT) reflect the effects of the specific causes X_i to effect Y. Node Y CPT defines the interaction of the particular causes X_i in producing effect Y. For Noisy - OR, node Y CPT is equivalent to deterministic OR CPT. The concept inhibitor nodes Y_i was introduced to represent the noise, or probabilistic effect y_i to Y. y_i 's CPT has the form:

$$P_r(y_i \mid x_i) = p_i$$

$$P_r(y \mid \bar{x}_i) = 0$$

p_i is the probability that the presence of x_i cause presence effect Y, and sometimes is called the causal power or formally presented

$p_i = P(y \mid \overline{x_1}, \overline{x_2}, ..., x_i, ..., \overline{x_n})$. Noisy-OR model assumes that the absence of X_i never produces the presence of Y. These assumptions allow the determination of the entire CPT for Y using only n parameters pi.

Oniško et al. (2001) gave the formula for the probability of event Y in case the subset is present $X_p \subseteq \{X_1, ..., X_n\}$

$$P(Y \mid X_p) = 1 - \prod_{i:X_i \in X_p} (1 - p_i) \tag{20}$$

representing a compact form of a conditional probability table. Of course, the possibility of constructing the CPT in this manner has its limitations and cannot be used on an arbitrary CPT Noisy-OR distribution.

Leaky Noisy-OR

In practice, it is quite impossible to incorporate all possible causes that can produce the effect into the model. Therefore, in practical models, the situation when the absence of all modeled causes guarantees absence of the effect is almost never happening. To address this weakness of Noisy-OR model, Henrion (1989) introduced the concept of a leak or background probability that allows modeling the impact of a combination of factors that are not in-

Figure 7. Direct modeling Noisy-OR
(Zagorecki & Druzdzel, 2013)

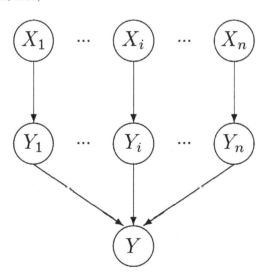

cluded in the model. The leaky Noisy-OR model can formally be presented using Noisy-OR. Leakage concept is implemented as an additional cause X_0 and its corresponds to inhibitor node Y_0. It is assumed that X_0 is always active and the probability that it will cause Y_0 is $\Pr(y_0 \mid x_0) = p_0$, where $0 < p_0 < 1$. Alternatively, leak as a binary variable X_0, with prior probability $\Pr(x_0) = p_0$ can be introduced, whose presence always produces the presence of Y.

Interpretation p_0 is the following: p_0 is the probability that the effect Y will happen even none of causes included in the model is present. It should be noted that the underlying assumption of the model is that unmodeled causes produce the effect independently of the modeled causes X_i.

Parameterization Leaky Noisy-OR

The introduction of a leak at the Noisy-OR model has interesting consequences from the model parameterization viewpoint. Noisy-OR parameter p_i corresponding to inhibitor Y_i is equal to the probability $p_i = P(y \mid \overline{x}_1, \overline{x}_2, ..., \overline{x}_i, ..., \overline{x}_n)$. When modeling Noisy-OR one does not have to explicitly ask about causal power of variable. Instead, it is possible to ask experts for the probability of event Y, provided that only one of the modeled causes is present and all the other causes are absent and thus implicitly calculate causal power. In addition, this approach enables using data directly from the database for learning Noisy-OR parameters. By extending the model to Leaky Noisy-OR, this approach is no longer valid. This is consequence of the assumption that the leakage happens unnoticed (Zagorecki & Druzdzel, 2004). Leaky Noisy-or CPT can be represented by:

$$P(\overline{Y} \mid X) = (1 - p_0) \prod_{i \in [1,n]} (1 - p_i) \tag{21}$$

where n is the number of parent nodes that have an effect to Y (Diez & Druzdzel, 2007).

Criteria for the use of the model OR

To apply the model in practice, the modeler must check the following criteria:

1. Are all the variables included in the model Boolean? For example, if one of the variables has categorical variable "sex", as parent OR model cannot be applied. It is not possible to connect one of its values (male and

female) as the cause of an anomaly, a different value with the absence of anomaly.

2. Is there a causal mechanism for each parent X, so that X can cause Y in the absence of other abnormalities? When the effect cannot be due to one cause or some combination of causes have to occur together to produce the effect, the model cannot be applied.

3. What is the nature of causal mechanisms? If some of these causal mechanisms are not deterministic, Noisy-OR model is used instead of deterministic OR model. If there are other causes which can cause Y that are not explicitly modeled, Leaky Noisy-OR model is used instead of Noisy-OR.

4. Are causal mechanisms independent? Compliance with this requirement is, in principle, the most difficult to establish, because of our domain knowledge, often is not precise enough to determine that the causal mechanisms and their inhibitors have no interaction. In practice, unless there is well-known interaction, it can be assumed that this condition is met and that the Noisy / Leaky – OR models can be applied. If this assumption does not stand, then one should use a non-ICI models, such as RNOR inhibited RNOR models.

5. Prior using Leaky Noisy-OR model one should check whether the implicit causes Y and their "ancestors", independent of any explicit variables in the model? Typically, it is assumed that this condition is met unless there is evidence against it.

If all the above conditions are satisfied, modeling can continue estimating numerical parameters, either from the database or experts. If expert ellcitation is used as a source for parameters estimation, and the cause X_i almost always produces an effect, it is recommended to ask an expert to assess the probability that an inhibitor prevents X_i from causing Y. It is much easier, for the expert, to give estimate whether the impact is 0.01 or 0.001 (the last is ten times greater than previous) than to choose among 0.99 or 0.999 (a difference of less than 1%) (Diez & Druzdzel, 2007).

APPLICATION OF BAYESIAN METHODS IN DECISION-MAKING

The most interesting results of the application of BBN in real world applications are related to calculating posterior probabilities for variables representing a problem that is to be solved (e.g., a possible diagnosis). These probabilities could be combined with the costs and benefits of taking one or more actions to address the problem, often represented in monetary terms. Using the outcome probability, caused by an action and a monetary value of a particular outcome, the expected value for every possible option in decision-making can be calculated. Usually, actions which produce the highest expected value are chosen. Sikavica et al. (2014) quoted the following core methods used for modeling under uncertainty and risk: decision trees, risk matrix, and sensitivity analysis. Many other studies have demonstrated that influence diagrams are an important tool in the application of Bayesian approach in decision making. In the next section, it will be described in more detail the expected utility theory, decision trees, and influence diagrams.

THE EXPECTED UTILITY THEORY

Managing availability typically involves decision making under uncertainty. When modeling this type of decision one should take into account the structure of the user's preference, how user compares the different results of its actions. In the case of availability management, the main dilemma is how to determine the level of investment in information systems to increase the availability facing potential threats to availability. The hardest investment decisions are in controls to protect from the threats that have a low frequency of occurrence and can have large consequences for the organization. A different attitude towards risk acceptance will lead to a different decision. The expected utility theory developed by von Neumann and Morgenstern is often used for making a decision in uncertain conditions. A brief overview of the basic details of the theory will be given. More information about the theory can be found in the von Neuman and Morgenstern's seminal work (Neumann & Morgenstern, 1947).

Let W be a set of possible outcomes of the lottery and w_i is one outcome in term expressed as monetary gain. Lottery L is defined as $\{(w_1, P_1), (w_2, P_2), \ldots (w_n, P_n)\}$ where P_i is the probability of an outcome w_i. Von Neumann and Morgenstern theory suggest that, if the structure satisfies the preferences set of particular primitive axioms (completeness, transitivity, continuity, and independence), then L_1 is preferred to L_2, if and only if vNMU (L_1)> vNMU (L_2), where:

$$vNMU(L) = \sum_n^i P_i * vNMU(w_i) \qquad (22)$$

is expected utility function according to von Neumann-Morgenstern's expected utility theory. In other words, the one lottery has the advantage over the other, if and only if it has a higher expected utility than another lottery. Based on this theory, decision-making becomes a process of finding an alternative with the maximum expected utility. Function vNMU is monotonously increasing function which represents the level of wealth w. The function intuitively reflects how satisfied decision-maker with the current level of wealth is.

Consider a utility function U(w) dependent of the variable w, representing wealth. Let's define marginal utility as MU (w) = dU(w)/dw. For each person, regardless of the approach, it is natural to assume that the MU(w)> 0 since the utility increases with the amount of wealth possessed. Personal risk appetite can determined, based on marginal utility, in the following way

- dMU(w)/dw>0 risks prone person. In other words, the additional value that person gets from one more dollar is higher when a person initially has a greater amount of wealth. This type of person tends to pay more attention to the potential value that can get by taking risks, than to the possible consequences.
- dMU(w)/dw<0 risks averse person. In other words, the added value brought by the new dollar value decreases with increasing wealth. An individual who avoids risk cares more about of the consequences of risk-taking than the value he can get by taking the risk.
- dMU(w)/dw=0 – risk neutral person. In other words, the added value does not depend on the amount of wealth. These people equally value the benefits and consequences of risk-taking (Cai, 2008).

Approaches toward risk may explain why people buy insurance even though premiums they pay are usually much larger than expected loss in case of the insured event (the person who avoids risks). It also clarifies the reason why people buy lottery although the money spent on the lottery is usually much higher than the expected value of lottery (person prone to risk). Based on numerous studies, Tversky and Kahneman (1979) have shown that people usually do not make decisions that maximize expected value.

Decision Trees

Decision trees are a graphical tool for modeling and evaluation of the decision-making process which consists of a series of decisions with uncertain consequences. A decision tree is composed of nodes and branches. There are two types of nodes: decision nodes represented by squares and random vari-

Figure 8. Utility functions for different risk-taking approaches
(French, Maule, & Papamichail, 2009)

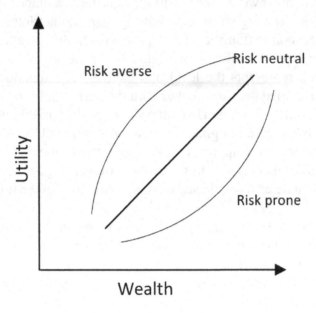

able nodes (various circumstances that have uncertain outcome) represented by circles. Squares are a representation of decisions which decision maker have to make. Branches coming out decision nodes are choices. The decision maker may choose only one alternative. The branches that are coming out from each circle node indicate the possible outcomes of this uncertain events. Every branch that emanates from the random variable node has associated probability meaning a chance that alternative will happen.

The biggest benefit of the decision tree method is the fact that, by calculation the profit of each alternative multiplied by their associated probabilities and comparing the resulting totals of all possible alternatives, it is possible to find one with maximum result. The process of aggregation is repeated, along with the path, until the decision maker is not able to identify the decisions that should be made by the initial node and subsequent decision nodes. The most common metric used in the method of the decision tree is the expected monetary value (Expected Monetary Value-EMV), which maximizes the expected cash return as a criterion for evaluating alternatives. It is possible to replace metric and instead a monetary value use subjective value, which measures the preferences of decision makers in the interval scale. In that case goal of the decision maker is to maximize the Expected utility-EU instead of maximizing EMV.

Decision trees are particularly useful in situations of complex multistage decision problems. For example, when it is needed to plan and organize a multilpe decisions in a way that, when making decisions take into account the choices made in the earlier stages, and take into account the outcomes of possible external events relevant to the decision-making process. A decision tree is essentially a diagram that represents decisions or other major external events that bring uncertainty in the decision-making process, by using the specially organized manner, as well as the possible outcomes of all these decisions and events. The Figure 9 shows a schematic example illustrating the basic elements of the decision tree.

Decision trees evaluate variables in sequential order determining the value of information with the aim of finding the most profitable solution for the organization. Also, this model encodes the structure of the decision problem representing all possible sequences of decisions and observations explicitly in the model (Jensen & Nielsen, 2007).

Analysis of decision problem using decision tree includes five steps:

1. Problem definition.
2. Structuring or constructing decision tree.
3. Assigning probabilities to random variable nodes.

Figure 9. A decision tree

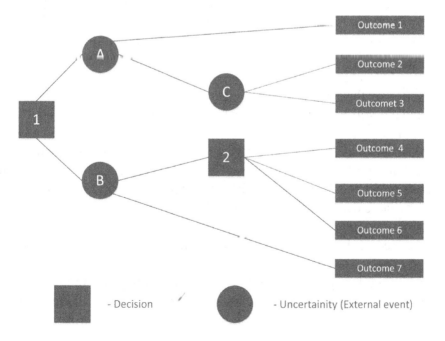

4.   Assessment of the cost-effectiveness of each possible combination of alternatives and states of nature.

5.   Solving tree by calculating the expected monetary value (EMV) for each random variable.

The procedure is applied by working backward, starting from the right end of the tree and working back toward to the nodes on the left. At each node, decision maker selects an alternative which has the highest EMV (Render, STAIR, & HANNA, 2012).

Advantages and Disadvantages of Decision Trees

Decision trees show all alternatives and their consequences which the decision-makers face. Also, the decision flow is moving chronologically from left to right, making a manager easier to follow the methodology. Tree-making can help the decision-maker to understand what should be included and what excluded from the tree. Another advantage is that the decision tree can help decision makers to understand the situation better and be able to describe it in others, leading to fewer errors. Finally, a decision tree encourages decision makers to solve a challenging problem of quantifying uncertainty and values that define decision.

An expected values analysis is the powerful framework for solving problems which include decisions under the risk but has some limitations. One of the constraints is related to the impossibility of modeling portfolio effect arising from the decision makers' attitude when this attitude is changing dynamically. Another limitation is the famous Allais paradox, where people sometimes violate, maximizing expected value principle, as a fundamental assumptions of the decision trees approach. The most commonly used criterion in practice is still EMV maximization although this method does not reflect the decision maker's risk appetite. Using EMV as criteria is acceptable only if the decision-maker is neutral to risks taking, which is rare (Fineman, 2010).

The main drawback of decision trees method is that tree grow exponentially with the number of decision variables and even very small problems require relatively large decision tree (Jensen & Nielsen, 2007) (Linnes, 2006).

It also often happens that the decision tree analyst is not paying attention to the entire tree. It is important to analyze all branches detail, otherwise, the method may lead to incorrect decisions and conclusions. Also, many people focus only on the one branch, for which they feel that has the largest possibility of profit or loss, leading to the incomplete decision-making process. The tree requires careful thought process (Linnes, 2006).

Influence Diagrams

The concept of Bayesian networks can be expanded with two new nodes type: a decision node and a value node. The decision node represents alternatives in decision making, and the value node represents the decision maker's preferences. The outcome of value node may depend on the random variables and the decision variables.

Resulting graphs are called influence diagrams and are used to calculate the expected value based on the decisions made and the observations that change values of random variables. Influence diagrams give a graphical representation of decisions structure, state of the environment in which a decision is made at one point in time. All details (alternative outcomes, consequences) are present in conditional probabilities tables that are assigned to the nodes. Influence diagram concept is an effective framework for modeling, presentation, and analysis decision under uncertainty, based on Bayes theorem. Influence diagrams bring a natural representation of the decision semantics making it the least clutter and confusion for decision-makers. Solving an influence diagram helps in determining the optimal strategy that maximizes the expected value and (or) calculate the maximum expected value in case of compliance with a chosen strategy.

An influence diagram is the type of causal model that differs from the Bayesian network. Bayesian network is a probabilistic network for reasoning under uncertainty, while the influence diagram helps in the decision-making under uncertainty. An influence diagram is a graph showing the structure of the decision problem which involves a series of interrelated decisions and observations. Similar to Bayesian networks, influence diagram is compact and intuitive probabilistic tool for knowledge representation (probabilistic networks). It consists of a network that describes the dependency relationships between entities in the problem domain, shows the order in which decisions are made. Also, there is a quantitative component representing the strength of dependency relations and decision maker's preferences. As such, influence diagram can be considered as a Bayesian network expanded with the decision variables, a utility function that specifies decision maker's preferences and the order of decisions making. Decision-makers are interested in the selection of the best possible decisions concerning modeled problem domain. Therefore, utility value is associated with the states of the network configuration. These values are represented by utility functions (also known as value function). The utility function assigns values to each configuration of domain variables. The goal of the analysis is to identify the decision-making options that produce the highest expected utility. Making decisions cause a change of conditional probabilities that are part of the network configuration. For the identification of decisions combination with the highest expected utility, it is necessary to calculate the expected utility of each alternative. If a decision with options $a_1, a_2, ..., a_m$, H is the hypothesis with the states $h_1, h_2, ..., h_n$ and ε is a set of observations in the form of evidence, then the value of each hypothesis outcome and the expected utility of every action can be calculated. The value of the outcome (a_i, h_j) is $U(a_i, h_j)$ where U () represents utility function. Expected utility function after taking action and is represented as

$$EU(a_i) = U(a_i, h_j)P(h_j \mid \varepsilon) \qquad (23)$$

where P () represents the decision maker's belief in H with given ε. The utility function U () encodes decision maker's preferences in numerical values. The combination of the actions, which has the highest expected utility should be selected as a solution to the problem. This method of selection of decision alternatives is known as the maximizing the expected utility principle. Choice of action a * that maximizes the expected utility can be expressed as

$$a^* = \arg\max_{a \in A} EU(a) \qquad (24)$$

There is a substantial difference between observation and action. Observation is a passive event in the sense that it is assumed that observation does not affect the state of the world while making the action is active in the meaning that action causes an event. The event caused by the making a decision may or may not be included in the model, depending on whether the event is relevant for drawing conclusions. If the event is caused by the action of A included in the model then A is called the intervening, otherwise, action A is non-intervening (Kjaerulff & Madsen, 2008). The easiest mistake one can make in understanding and building influence diagrams is to interpret it as flow charts. Flowchart describes the sequential nature of the particular process in which each node represents an event or activity. Although influence diagram looks a bit like flowcharts, it is fundamentally different. The influence diagram is a snapshot of decisions at some point, which should take into account all the elements of decisions that influence direct decision-making. Assigning a random variable to a node in the influence diagram means that although the decision maker is not sure what will happen, he or she has some idea of the probabilities of different possible outcomes (Clemen & Reilly, 2003).

If decision node is added to the Bayesian network dealing with server availability problem (see Figure 6) with possible decisions {nothing, replace_hardware, restore} and utility function, which depends on the state of nodes OS_error and Hardware_failure and decision node "Action" an influence diagram shown in Figure 10 will be constructed.

In the diagram, shown on the Figure 10, edges, that connect nodes "Update_last_night" and "Server_available" and decision node "action", means that the state of these variables is known before making an action decision.

Table 4 represents the utility function for the example problem of the server availability in which the value of 1 denotes combination values of variables OS_error, Hardware_failure, Action, which should solve the problem. Otherwise the function has value 0. If the server is inaccessible, but it is found that the last night made an update of the operating system, or variable Server_available = No and variable Update_last_night = "updated", the expected value for all possible of decisions is shown in the table below.

Figure 10. Influence diagram for the server availability problem example

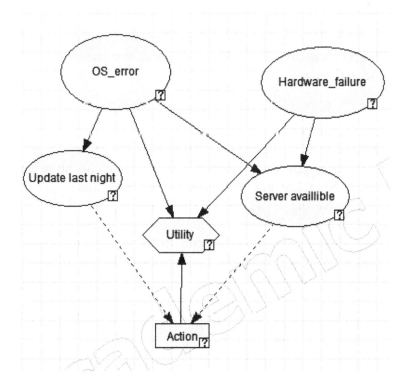

Table 4. Utility function for the server availability problem example

		Action		
OS_Error	Hardware_Failure	No_Action	Replace_Hardware	Restore
1	1	0	1	1
1	0	0	0	1
0	1	0	1	0
0	0	1	0	0

Using the principle of maximizing expected utility based on these values, OS should be restored from backup because expected value for this is highest.

In general, the scope of the function is represented by a set of real numbers. If the value of the utility function is expressed in monetary units, the expected value of possible decisions can be directly interpreted as a monetary gain or loss.

Instances of the Use of Probabilistic Networks

There are many good reasons for choosing probabilistic networks as a framework to solve problems of making decisions under uncertainty. As mentioned above, some of them are:

- Coherent and mathematically supported management of uncertainty,
- Normative decisions,
- Automatic construction and adaptation model based on the data,
- Intuitive and compact representation of causal relationships and (conditional) dependence and independence relations, and
- Efficient answering to the queries based on the given evidence.

However, there are some requirements that the problem must fulfill in order to be able to apply probabilistic networks models to it. Some key requirements are listed below:

Table 5.

	No_action	Restore	Replace_hardware
EU	0.03	0.97	0.003

- The variables and events (i.e. possible values of variables) of the problem must have a well-defined domain
- One must have knowledge about the causal relationship between variables, conditional probabilities that quantify the relationships and values (preferences) associated with different decisions options.
- Uncertainty should be presented in at least some relationship between the variables.
- The problem to be solved should contain an element of the decision including the desire to increase the expected utility of the decision.

Data is often available in the form of common observation of subset variables related to the problem domain. Each set of common observations refers to a specific instance (case) the problem domain. For example, a data source can be a database of customers, where each record (case), has many attributes (e.g., gender, age, marital status, income, etc.). Structure and parameters of the probabilistic network can be constructed using statistical analysis of available data. These automatically generated models can reveal much information about dependence and independence relations (and sometimes even the causal mechanisms) among the variables, and thus provide new knowledge about the problem domain. Sometimes, however, there is no enough available data for making a clear and consistent link between the variables or patterns of interaction between the variables are highly complex. In such cases, the model based on the neural networks may be a better alternative. This model consists of a function that attempts to match each input case with the desired output using iterative adjustment of a large number of coefficients (weights) until convergence (i.e., while the distance between the desired and actual output becomes small enough) (Kjaerulff & Madsen, 2008).

SENSITIVITY ANALYSIS

After finishing construction of influence diagram, the next step is called "analysis phase". Although the process of creating the diagram focuses on the institutional knowledge and therefore experts' verifications are required, the analysis phase provides critical insight into this knowledge and directs the modeling. A set of analytical tools for the analysis includes a nominal sensitivity analysis, parameter sensitivity analysis, stochastic analysis, and calculation of the value of information.

Nominal sensitivity analysis is a filtering technique for identifying key variables that have the greatest impact on the decision. Estimates are made between the upper and lower bounds for all variables, usually between 10 and 90 percent variable range. The objective function is calculated for each variable, between two limits, while all other variables have fixed values. In general, variables that are found to have the greatest impact on the target function, during sensitivity analysis, are selected for further analysis and potentially a more detailed characterization in the subsequent iterations of the modeling process. For a nominal analysis "tornado diagram" is often used (Figure 11). The main advantage of a tornado diagram is that it shows the significance of the impact of the variables on the objective function, as well as the sensitivity of the model to the changes in value of an analyzed variable. The graph presented in Figure 11 prioritizes variables according to the impact strength, showing on the top variables, whose variability has the biggest influence on the function value.

The parametric sensitivity analysis, as w its name suggests, parameterizes particular variable and examines how the optimal decision is changed in response to changes in input variable. A key interest in this type of analysis is the "point of transition", where the best decision changes from one alternative to another. This sensitivity analysis provides insight into the ro-

Figure 11. Tornado diagram

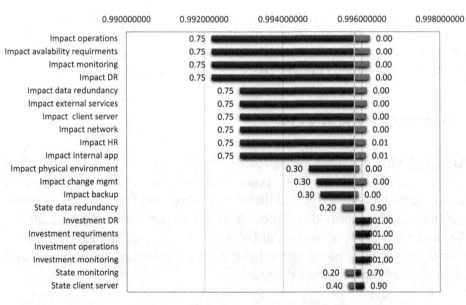

bustness of the chosen alternative. If the decision about the best alternative changes with small variations of a particular input variable, then this variable should be subject to more detailed modeling and data collection.

Once the relevant variables in the sensitivity analysis are identified, the stochastic analysis examines the role of uncertainty in the decision. The techniques based on the rules of stochastic dominance are used for ranking of alternative decisions. Full statistical distribution of utility function is a foundation for decision-making, based on the decision maker's preferences. The stochastic dominance of the first, second and third degree are successively applied for improving the precision of the criteria used for assessing superiority among alternative decisions. Details on the mathematical settings related to these criteria can be found in the work of Kevin Hoo (Hoo, 2000).

MONTE – CARLO SIMULATION

Monte-Carlo methods are stochastic simulation methods or algorithms which, by using random or pseudo-random number generator and a large number of calculations and repetitions, may predict the behavior of the complex mathematical system. Monte - Carlo method uses a probabilistic calculation algorithm where the value of one or more random variables is given by the density function. It aims at predicting all possible process outcomes with probability of their occurrence. As such, the Monte-Carlo method proves to be extremely useful in the process of decision making under risk. The value of the Monte-Carlo algorithm is in fact that, as a final result, it gives all possible outcomes, including the probability of occurrence of each of these results. Furthermore, by using the results of the Monte-Carlo simulation, it is feasible to conduct a sensitivity analysis to identify the factors with the greatest influence on the process outcome.

The algorithm can be explained as follows:

1. Create mathematical model of the business process,
2. Find variables whose values are not completely certain,
3. Find density functions that adequately describe distributions of random variables,
4. If there are correlations among the variables, make the correlation matrix,
5. In each iteration assign a random value, using density function, to each variable taking into account the correlation matrix,

6.   Calculate output value and save results,
7.   Repeat steps five and six n times, and
8.   Statistically analyze the simulation results (Masle & Crnjac Milić, 2013).

Conrad (Conrad, 2005) used the Monte-Carlo simulation in information security analysis. The security model is treated as a function that accepts a set of parameters and returns a set of forecasted results. Instead of supplying a single set of fixed parameter values directly to the security model, an analyst defines a set of random variable distributions (based on the experts' assessments) using a Monte-Carlo tool. The tool selects a random value for each parameter, executes security model with these values, and collects modeling results to the output distribution.

In other words, the simulation randomly selects a value for each parameter, thousands of times and calculates the results according to a given model. However, applying Monte – Carlo simulation demands additional information from the experts, which should give the probability distribution of the model variable. This request could be problematic because of the unwillingness of experts for assessing distribution (experts in security usually do not have enough skills to describe the statistical distribution), as well as the length of the elicitation process (Panchit, 2009).

Figure 12. Applying Monte - Carlo method in information security

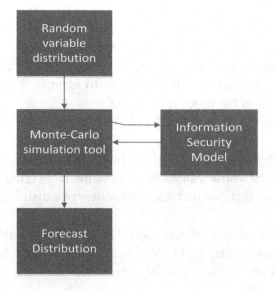

REAL WORLD CASES

De Bruyckere, V., Systemic Risk Rankings and Network Centrality in the European Banking Sector, September 2015

This paper presents a methodology to calculate the Systemic Risk Ranking of financial institutions in the European banking sector using publicly available information. The proposed model makes use of the network structure of financial institutions by including the stock return series of all listed banks in the financial system. Furthermore, a wide set of common risk factors (macroeconomic risk factors, sovereign risk, financial risk and housing price risk) is included to allow these factors to affect the banks. The model uses Bayesian Model Averaging (BMA) of Locally Weighted Regression models (LOESS), i.e. BMA-LOESS. The network structure of the financial sector is analyzed by computing measures of network centrality (degree, closeness and betweenness) and it is shown that this information can be used to provide measures of the systemic importance of institutions. Using data from 2005 (2nd quarter) to 2013 (3rd quarter), this paper provides further insight into the time-varying importance of risk factors and it is shown that the model produces superior conditional out-of-sample forecasts (i.e. projections) than a classical linear Bayesian multi-factor model. Available at: https://www.ecb.europa.eu/pub/pdf/scpwps/ecbwp1848.en.pdfhttps://papers.ssrn.com/sol3/papers.cfm?abstract_id=2664152

Bloomberg, J., Three-Way Big Data Banking Battle Brewing, July 29, 2014

Ensuring all the data internal to the organization is on the up-and-up requires that they analyze both the data and the data quality information that it generates, and traditional analytical approaches – even Big Data analytics – leave holes the bad actors can penetrate.

As a result, some banks are moving past such analytics technologies into new areas based on probability and inductive, heuristic logic. "Emerging approaches toward money laundering detection try to replicate the dynamic thought processes of an expert analyst," according to a CEB Towergroup report. "Studies have shown that in situations where information is too limited for a person to make a logical choice, humans follow a heuristic or experience-based approach to decision making. In this method the human brain draws on a variety of sparse, interrelated contextual data leveraged from past experiences to establish strong inferences about a decision."

In order to calculate such inferences, banks use Bayesian Belief Networks (BBNs). According to CEB Towergroup, "In AML management, BBN models determine whether a set of transactions should be flagged high risk, not only by matching it to a known scenario, but also by considering contextual information such as customer demographics, risk profile, and account type." As a result, the Bayesian models can identify money laundering transactions as suspicious within the broader context of other information relevant to the transactions Available at: http://www.forbes.com/sites/jasonbloomberg/2014/07/29/three-way-big-data-banking-battle-brewing/#2573f1234fe4

CHAPTER SUMMARY

In this chapter, the concept of Bayesian Belief Networks (BBN) was introduced. The process of BBN construction was also explained. Noisy-OR model was introduced as a way to overcome the problem of the big number of parameters (conditional probabilities) needed for a BBN model parameterization. The basic assumption for introducing Noisy-Or model is that there is no correlation between causes (independent variables) and that each cause, independently of the other, may induce the result (the dependent variable). Henrion (Henrion, 1989) introduced Leaky Noisy-OR mode, to include the influence of variables that were not included explicitly in Nosy-OR model. In Leaky Noisy-OR model, the leak probability was introduced as the probability that result would happen even if all modelled casu are not active. In following part of the chapter, the application of Bayesian logic in the decision-making process was presented. Norman Morgenstern utility theory was explained as a theoretical basis for the decision-making process in the modeled problem. Influence diagrams and Decision trees are presented as tools for an implementation of the utility theory and necessary conditions for an application of probabilistic models in a decision-making process were explained. Sensitivity analysis is introduced as an important technique for assessing the impact of particular variables on the decision. The chapter contains a brief explanation of the Monte Carlo simulation method. Monte Carlo is stochastic simulation method or algorithm which, by using random or pseudo-random number generator and a large number of calculations and repetitions, may predict the behavior of the complex mathematical system. The steps for the execution of simulation and cases of use in the field of information security and operational risks were also presented in this chapter.

REFERENCES

Alexander, C. (2003). Managing operational risks with Bayesian networks. *Operational Risk: Regulation. Analysis and Management, 1*, 285–294.

Cai, Z. (2008). *Risk-based proactive availability management-attaining high performance and resilience with dynamic self-management in Enterprise Distributed Systems* [Doctoral dissertation]. Georgia Institute of Technology.

Clemen, R. T., & Reilly, T. (2013). *Making hard decisions with Decision-Tools*. Cengage Learning.

Conrad, J. (2005). Analyzing the risks of information security investments with Monte-Carlo simulations. *Proceedings of the Workshop on the Economics of Information Security*.

Darwiche, A. (2010). Bayesian networks. *Communications of the ACM, 53*(12), 80–90. doi:10.1145/1859204.1859227

Diez, F. J., & Druzdzel, M. J. (2006). *Canonical probabilistic models for knowledge engineering* (Technical Report CISIAD-06-01). UNED.

Ding, J. (2010). Probabilistic inferences in Bayesian networks. In A. Rebai (Ed.), *Bayesian Network* (pp. 39–53). doi:10.5772/46968

Fineman, M. (2010). *Improved Risk Analysis for Large Projects: Bayesian Networks Approach*. Queen Mary, University of London.

French, S., Maule, J., & Papamichail, N. (2009). *Decision Behaviour, Analysis and Support*. Cambridge University Press. doi:10.1017/CBO9780511609947

Gran, B. (2002). Use of Bayesian Belief Networks when combining disparate sources of information in the safety assessment of software-based systems. *International Journal of Systems Science, 33*(6), 529–542. doi:10.1080/00207720210133589

Henrion, M. Some Practical Issues in Constructing Belief Networks. *Proc. 3rd Conf. on Uncertainty in Artificial Intelligence* (pp. 161-173). Elsevier.

Hoo, K. J. S. (2000). *How much is enough? A risk management approach to computer security*. Stanford, Calif: Stanford University.

Jensen, F. V., & Nielsen, T. D. (2009). *Bayesian networks and decision graphs*. Springer Science & Business Media.

Kahneman, D., & Tversky, A. (1979). Prospect Theory: An Analysis of Decision under Risk. *Econometrica*, *47*(March), 263–291. doi:10.2307/1914185

Kjaerulff, U., & Madsen, A. L. (2008). *Bayesian Networks and Influence Diagrams: A Guide to Construction and Analysis*. Springer Science + Business Media, LLC.

Linnes, C. (2006). *Applying Decision Theory to Quantify the Cost of Network Security Risk*. Nova Southeastern University.

Masle, D., & Crnjac Milić, D. (2013). *Mogucnost primjene monte carlo metode na primjeru agroekonomskog problema prilikom donosenja odluka u uvjetima rizika*. Ekonomski Vjesnik.

Neil, M., Marquez, D., & Fenton, N. (2008). Using Bayesian networks to model the operational risk to information technology infrastructure in financial institutions. *Journal of Financial Transformation*, *22*, 131–138.

Neumann, J., & Morgenstern, O. (1947). *Theory of games and economic behavior* (2nd ed.). Princeton University Press.

Oniśko, A., Druzdzel, M. J., & Wasyluk, H. (2001). Learning Bayesian network parameters from small data sets: Application of Noisy-OR gates. *International Journal of Approximate Reasoning*, *27*(2), 165–182. doi:10.1016/S0888-613X(01)00039-1

Panchit, P. (2009). *Quantified Return on Information Security Investment - a Model for Cost-Benefit Analysis*. Delft University of Technology.

Pearl, J. (2014). *Probabilistic reasoning in intelligent systems: networks of plausible inference*. Morgan Kaufmann.

Render, B., Stair, R. M., & Hanna, M. E. (2012). *Quantitative Analysis For Management* (11th ed.). Prentice Hall.

Sikavica, P., Hunjak, T., Begičević-Redžep, N., & Hernaus, T. (2014). *Poslovno odlučivanje*. Zagreb: Školska knjiga.

Yu, Y., Zheng, G., & Qian, Z. (2009, November). Software Reliability Model Analysis Including Internal Structure Based on Bayesian Network. *Proceedings of the Fourth International Conference on Cooperation and Promotion of Information Resources in Science and Technology COINFO'09* (pp. 247-251). IEEE. doi:10.1109/COINFO.2009.82

Zagorecki, A., & Druzdzel, M. J. (2004, May). An Empirical Study of Probability Elicitation Under Noisy-OR Assumption. Proceedings of Flairs conference (pp. 880-886).

Zagorecki, A., & Druzdzel, M. J. (2013). Knowledge engineering for Bayesian networks: How common are noisy-MAX distributions in practice? *IEEE Transactions on Systems, Man, and Cybernetics, Systems, 43*(1), 186–195.

Chapter 5
Application of BBN in Information Systems and Operational Risk Management

ABSTRACT

In this chapter, the model used to measure and maximize IS availability is described. The method of selecting independent variables will be presented, with a detailed definition of each variable in the model. This section presents a model based on Bayesian network, utility theory and influence diagrams. Finally, a method for probability elicitation through an interview with domains experts will be described, as recommended data collection model, for cases where it is not possible to set parameter' values based on learning from data.

LITERATURE REVIEW

Weber et al. (2012) presented a bibliographic review of BBN applications in reliability, risk analysis and maintenance domains for the period 2002-2012 and showed that number of articles has a rising trend. They analyzed some 200 references in the field of application of BBN in reliability, risk analysis, and application maintenance, examining a database with over 7,000 BBN references. As one of the main reasons for such a growing trend, they attributed to strengths of Bayesian networks, compared to other classical methods of reliability analysis such as Markov chains, Fault trees, and Petri Nets. Some of these advantages are: the ability to model complex systems, capacity to use BBN for prediction and diagnosis, ability to calculate the

DOI: 10.4018/978-1-5225-2268-3.ch005

exact probability of occurrence of an event and update the calculation on the basis of new evidence, the possibility of presenting multimodal variables and tools for modeling, and compact graphical display of a modeled problems.

Franke et al. (2012) presented a model for decision support in the area of availability of information systems based on BBN. The model parameters are obtained based on the opinions of 50 experts in the area of availability of information systems. Raderius et al. (2009) presented a case study where the availability of the information system was estimated using "extended influence diagrams" - a form of BBN- combined with the architectural metamodel. Hinz and Malinowski (2006) presented the BBN model of IT infrastructure risk. The parameters of this model are obtained using interviews with experts. Weber and Sumner (2001) used the influence diagrams for the economic analysis of information systems availability. Neil et al. (2009) presented a methodology for developing BBN model for managing the operational risk of IT infrastructure in the financial and other institutions. The presented methodology enables modeling of financial losses that may arise as a result of operational risks, including data centers, applications, systems and processes, and in particular services to clients that are supported by information technology. Wei et al. (2011) developed an integrated modeling process based on the BBN for supporting efficient management of IT services. Sommestad and Ekstedt (2009) suggested a model based on the extended influence diagram, which allows the analysis of the cyber security of different architectural solutions. The model supports the selection of the appropriate scenarios, based on relative prices of a countermeasures against loss resulting from the attack. Cemerlic et al. (2008) proposed an intrusions detection system (IDS) based on BBN. Simonsson et al. (2008) proposed a model for measuring the quality of managing information technologies based on BBN. The model was validated in 35 different organizations. Lande et al. (2010) modeled critical information systems by using a BBN model that improves the system resilience by predicting possible failures of the system components. Zhang et al. (2009) presented an innovative model to improve the information system availability based on the BBN in which the data for filling CPT are obtained from system logs. In a review of the statistical methods that can be used for modeling of business continuity management, Bonafede and Cerchiello (2007) provided examples on how to use BBN for this purpose. Linnes (2006) suggested using decision theory for quantifying the costs of network security risks, and presented models based on influence diagrams and decision trees.

Different models based on BBN approach were suggested in the area of software reliability (Yu et al., 2009) (Dejaeger & Verbraken, 2012) (Gran,

2002), software development project management (Fenton, Hearty, Neil, & Radliński, 2010) (Fenton et al., 2004) (Fineman, 2010) (Radliński, Fenton, & Neil, 2007). Microsoft founded one of the first research centers for Bayesian networks. Their algorithm for solving printing problems is based on BBN, it is described by Heckerman (1995)Yoon (2003) and Adusei-Poku (2005) used BBN for modeling operational risk in a financial institution.

Wang and Mosleh (2010) presented a framework for expansion of BBN, which allows the use of both qualitative and quantitative scale for measuring probability in the construction of Bayesian networks. The inclusion of qualitative scale is particularly useful when there is no quantitative data to assess the probability and experts are reluctant to express their opinions quantitatively. In the area of reliability and risk analysis, this is a common problem when human and organizational causes of systems failures are explicitly modeled. Such causes often cannot be quantified due to technical limitations and the lack of adequate quantitative metrics.

Dejaegere & Verbraken (2012) identified the process of software testing as a key activity in the software development life cycle and provided a literature review based research, looking for examples of using BBN for a software failure predictions. Results of this study showed that, in this particular domain, the use of "Naive Bayes classifier" is prevailing, referring to the predictive performance and user-friendliness as a major advantage. They tested 15 different Bayesian Network (BN) classifiers and compared them to other popular machine learning techniques.

Doguc (2010) proposed a BBN-based methodology for assessing the reliability, sensitivity analysis and diagnosis of failures in complex systems. Such probabilistic approach is used to model and predict the behavior of a system based on the observation of stochastic events. A complex system is defined as any system with a large number of interactions of components and assumed that these systems are composed of different subsystems. Also, he suggested holistic methods for the automated construction of BBN models for assessing the reliability of complex systems.

Fenton et al. (2012) addressed the problem of reliability assessment in a complex system. They explored breakdowns of the system components and researched how system design affects the reliability of complex systems. They showed how BBN can be used to model a system reliability from data collection during the test or operation, how to forecast future reliability of the system or to diagnose errors in such systems. In addition, they showed how to take into account a system structure into the analysis, and how to use a special design that provides fault tolerance, redundancy and other methods to improve system reliability.

Fenton et al. (2001) pointed out that a large number of approaches for predicting a software quality exists but found none of them achieved widespread applicability. As a solution to this problem, they proposed a unique model that combines different forms, often causally related, of evidence available in software development process. During the model construction process, they used Bayesian networks and subjective assessment of experienced project manager as a data source. Resulting model can be used for forecasting software quality through the whole development lifecycle.

However, Fenton and Neil (2001) stated that there are many circumstances in which decisions must be made based on several criteria, and BBN approach does not address the concept of preference that is needed in such cases. Therefore, BBN method cannot, on its own, provide a complete solution for this kind of broader problems which include the issue of assessing system security. In such situations, BBN has to be combined with other decision-making techniques such as multi-criterion decision analysis (MCDA). They explained the role of BBN in making such decisions and described the general decision-making process by using BBN and MCDA in a complementary way.

Kondakci (2010) introduced a causal risk assessment methods (CRAM) based on BBN for identification and analysis of causal threats and quantifying risks associated with them.

Foroughi (2008) dealt with risk identification problem and evaluation of new information assets by their characteristics, current security controls and consequences before the incident. To solve this problem, he proposed a system that could help experts in risk assessment through regular business processes. The proposed system should be responsive and independent, as it should respond promptly and independently of events. The system is designed in the form of intelligent software agent that learns about the risks by experience about the risk factors and the assets' characteristics, predicts the risks probability for the new assets, and it is based on Bayesian learning techniques.

Houmb, Georg, & France (2005) studied the issue of risk-driven development (RDD) in which security risks are identified, evaluated and treated as an integral part of RDD. They developed a framework that deals with the choice of a treatment strategy for system security issues using cost-benefits analysis and trade-off analysis and calculating return on security investment (ROSI). ROSI is calculated as the ratio between the gain from security investment and costs of an investment in security weaknesses treatments. They identified four ways to increase the ROSI: minimize or eliminate losses, minimize investment, maximizing the benefits of return, the acceleration return time. Cost-benefits analysis and trade-off analysis as the main part of the framework are implemented using BBN.

Johnson, Lagerström, and associates (2007) suggested the use of formal language for supporting the analysis of enterprise architecture of an information system. They formed a set of requirements that such language should meet. After a thorough evaluation of several alternatives, they chose modified influence diagram as the most suitable. The resulting modified influence diagram is different from the conventional, regarding the built-in ability to cope with definitional uncertainties, i.e., uncertainties related to the use of language and their ability to represent multiple levels.

Lagerström Johnson et al. (2009) worked on the application of BBN to analyze software changes. The network contains a set of variables affecting the cost of making software changes both on the architectural and component level. An expert survey was conducted to find the strength of the effect between all the related variables.

Okutan and Yildiz (2012) made a research on the application of BBN in predicting software defects. They used Bayesian networks to determine the significant probabilistic relationships among software metrics and defect proneness.

BAYESIAN MODEL FOR ANALYZING AND MAXIMIZING INFORMATION SYSTEM AVAILABILITY

The main objective of the modeling process was to create a model which may help in maximizing information system availability and choosing optimal technical and organizational controls. Every investment option must meet at least one of the following two criteria:

1. Measurable financial benefits. For instance, in case of an investment in security systems, the benefit is measured through avoidance of potential losses.
2. Compliance with industry specific regulations which demand the introduction of specific systems and technologies.

Various mathematical models based on historical data are used for the prediction of the potential losses resulting from operational risks (including the risks related to IT technology). Many of these models predict well as losses incurred as a consequence of high frequency events and historical data is available. However, a major problem of models based on historical data is a lack of data on low frequency, but high impact events. Models based on probability are an adequate alternative, and Bayesian Belief Networks are often used as a tool for modeling information security and operational risks (Fenton & Neil, 2007) (Neil et al., 2008)(Foroughi, 2008) (Roshandel, Medvidovic, & Golubchik, 2007)(Franke et al., 2012).

VARIABLES AND THE MODEL CONSTRUCTION

Prior to the presentation of independent variables in the model, it is necessary to define the method of measuring the availability... As the system consists of several services oriented to both internal and external customers, overall system availability is defined as the average availability of each service weighted by a factor of importance of a service (for example different weight is given for a payment card authorization service and a service that calculates fixed assets depreciation). The equation (25) is used for the availability calculation.

$$A = \frac{\sum_i A_i * k_i}{\sum_i k_i} \tag{25}$$

In this formula A- represents overall system availability, Ai- an availability of service s_i and k_i – a coefficient significance of service s_i.

When calculating the availability of a particular service one should take into account the service operating time defined in the service level agreement, as well as the number of clients affected by the service interruption. The availability of a particular service is calculated according to the following formula:

$$A_i = \frac{t_i}{t_i + ut_i * \frac{un_i}{n_i}} \tag{26}$$

t_i is the total time that service s_i was available under service level agreement, ut_i - the total time for which the system was unavailable, n_i -the total number of the service users, un_i-the number of service users where experienced service interruption during time ut_i.

Dependent and Independent Variables

During the literature review, we identified the model developed by Franke et al. (2012) as a model which has very good fit with our research framework. Therefore, we decided to adapt this model for the purposes of this book. Initial model consisted of the following 14 variables: physical environment, requirements and procurement, operation, change control, technical solution of backup, process solution of backup, data and storage architecture redundancy, avoidance of internal application failures, avoidance of external services that fail, network redundancy, avoidance of network failures, physical location, resilient client/server solution, monitoring of relevant components.

The basis for the definition of a set of variables is the "availability index", which was introduced by Marcus and Stern (2003), shown in the following diagram (Figure 1).

Figure 1. Availability index
(Marcus & Stern, 2003)

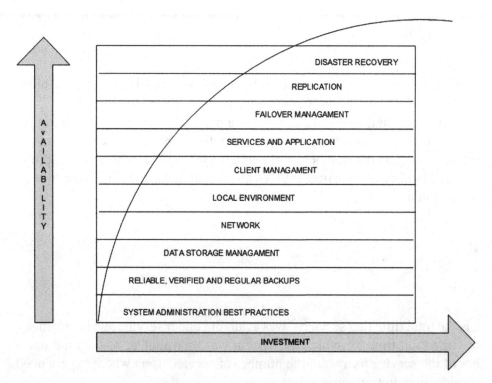

For every variable of the model, a thorough literature review has been made, in order to examine the best practices in the field and provide justification why it should be included in the model. Consequently, we merged the variables "technical solution of backup" and "process solution of backup", from the original model, into a variable "Backup management". Similarly, variables "network redundancy" and "avoidance of network failure" are merged into the variable "network management" (Ibrahimovic and Bajgoric 2016). Backup variables are not separated neither in "the availability index" nor in one of the other reference models (Marcus & Stern, 2003), (Raucsher, Krock, & RUNYON, 2006), (Bajgoric, 2008). In fact, if the organization sets high requirements on the RTO and RPO (as part of the process solution), that setting would determine the technical solution because there are only a few (or sometimes just one) solutions that meet these requirements. A similar argument can be made for merging the variables "network redundancy" and "avoidance of network failure". Network redundancy can be considered as one of the strategies to avoid a network failure, and a superset of both variables is network management.

Apart from this, another variable "Human resources management" has been added. The main reason for adding this variable to the model is in fact that in at least three models representing IS availability, human resources are considered an important factor that affects the IS availability (Marcus & Stern, 2003), (Raucsher et al., 2006), (Bajgoric, 2008). Additionally, as Gartner pointed out in its report related to Disaster Recovery and Data Replication Architectures 80% of unplanned downtime is caused by "people failures," and recommended "employment of quality and competent staff and their continuous training" (Scott, 2005). Final version of the model consisted of thirteen causal factors: physical environment, availability requirements management, operations management, change management, backup management, storage redundancy, avoiding errors in internal applications, avoiding errors in external services, network management, equipment and location of the DR data centre, resilient client/server systems, monitoring of relevant components, human resources management.

Since ITIL based explanations of these causal factors can be found In (Franke, Johnson, & König, 2014), with more details in the Ibrahimović's doctoral thesis (2016), only brief explanation emphasizing a practical aspect is given below.

Physical environment refers to data center's location and equipment. According to the ITIL definition (S. Taylor, Vernon, & Rudd, 2007) data center can refer to the main data centers, regional data centers, server rooms and other facilities that accommodate the communications and server equipment.

Due to the specificity of the practical part of this research, where there are companies that have a centralized infrastructure, this book will address only the main data centers. Many events may cause IS unavailability in case of non-applying best practices in, for instance if data center does not have two independent power sources secured by generators and UPS.

Availability requirements management represents the impact of an adequate definition of availability requirements, which an information system should achieve. Enterprise systems can vary significantly according to the availability requirements (Cai, 2008). The mistakes made at early stages of system design stage can be difficult to recover in the later stages, especially for systems that require continuous operations. Bauer (2010) distinguishes between two types of demands on system availability:

- High-level requirements that define the services availability in Service Level Agreement (SLA).
- Detailed requirements that determine the design and test scenarios for system testing.

High-level requirements need to answer three questions: Which cases of failure are covered (planned, unplanned)? Does the unavailability definition include only total system downtime or it covers partial outages as well? What is the requirement for the system availability on an annual basis, expressed as a percentage? Detailed requirements fall into one of four categories: behavior requirements, failure rate, latency requirements, and requirements on the probability of failure.

Operation management includes the following processes (S. Taylor, Cannon, & Wheldon, 2007),

- **Event Management:** Involves monitoring of all system events, to be able to identify and react to any unusual activity.
- **Incidents and Problems Management:** Incident management for a task has to return an IS service to the users as soon as possible and thus to reduce the impact on the business. Problem management, on the other hand, aims to find and eliminate the cause of incidents and undertake the preventive activities that prevent future incidents.
- **Service Requests Fulfillment:** Resolution of standard requirements that pass through service desk, which can be fulfilled without a formal change request (replacement of the standard pieces of equipment and similar).

- **Access Control:** Is facilitating the use of information resources and services to authorized users, while preventing access to unauthorized users. These are operations of manipulating user accounts and access rights at the request of the Human Resource Management Department.

Change management. ITIL defines change as: "the introduction, modification or removal of approved, maintained or basic hardware, network, software, application, environment, system, desktop or associated documentation". Change management is closely related to IS availability since one of the characteristics of poor change management is "unexpected interruption." Also, as the important indicator used to measure change management quality, ITIL states "no interruptions, incidents, problems/ errors caused by failure to change" (Taylor, Lacy & MacFarlane, 2007).

Backup is an additional copy of production data, created and kept specially for the purpose of recovery of lost or corrupted data (Gnanasundaram & Shrivastava, 2012). By introducing variable backup management we wanted to determine the extent to which applying the best practices in this area contribute to increasing IS availability. Continues data protection (CDP) is becoming more and more used in production environments (Gartner, 2011). Increasing in hard disk capacity as well as decreasing the price per stored GB lead to the use of disk for backup at a rapid rate (Castagna, 2013). Also, more and more companies are turning to cloud-based backup, especially for e-mail backup. All those technologies enable lower RTO and RPO times and improve system availability.

Storage Redundancy was considered from two aspects: data redundancy and storage architecture redundancy. Data redundancy describes the method used to encode and distribute data to more independent units of data storage to increase the resilience in case of failures and malicious attacks (Bakkaloğlu, Wylie, Wang et al., 2002). The techniques used for this purpose, among others, include RAID, local and remote data replication. The complete system architecture for data storage should contain redundant paths from the server to the disks. It includes redundant disk controllers, redundant network components that transmit data between servers and storage systems (switches and NICs / HBA). Another important aspect is choosing adequate storage architecture. Since an organization can make a choice between direct-attached storage (DAS), network area storage (NAS), storage area networks (SAN) for data storage (or combine them), it is important to consider all relevant criteria when choosing a solution.

Avoiding errors in internal applications is an imperative for IS availability. This implies the applications used in production environment, as well as the process of design, development and introduction of new applications. Ensuring software stability is an important task due to scalability and resilience requirements. The applications need to be available on continuous and always-on basis even in cases of increasing number of concurrent users, and constant changes in complex systems where a change in one system component (software, network, hardware) can affect the application's stability.

From the system availability viewpoint, it is necessary to put under control all processes in the application lifecycle. The process can be managed by a variety of techniques described in the standards for quality control ISO 9000, CMM (Capability Maturity Model), SPICE (Software Process Improvement and Capability Determination -ISO / IEC 15504), Bootstrap (Conradi & Fuggetta, 2002).

Avoiding errors in external services can also improve the system availability. In addition to communication and network services, the most important examples of external services in the financial system are systems for payment transactions settlement, systems for processing credit card transactions, maintenance and application development, design and maintenance of network and system infrastructure. Before organization decides to externalize an IT service or entire IT operations, it should take all necessary actions to avoid possible operational risks. Organization must have full control on externalized services as if they were performed within an organization. Before making decisions about externalization, the organization needs to fully understand the functioning of the services that are candidates for externalization. When selecting service providers, an organization has to assess capabilities, viability, reputation and risk management methods of prospective partners. The contract should clearly define the obligations of parties, a way of verifying the execution of duties, the responsibility for possible damages resulting from failure to comply with the contract.

Network management has a significant impact on IS availability. A survey conducted by Forrester showed that in large companies, data network issues caused on average, 15% of all problems on IS availability. However, only 2% are due to the actual fault of the networking equipment. The remaining 13% are due to various problems such as human error, unmanaged changes, misconfigurations, routing problems and problems with network software (Mendel, 2004). There are different techniques for increasing network availability. One of them is using redundant network components such as switches, routers, security appliances as well as all key network services (DNS, DHCP, LDAP, RADIUS, IDP). Ideally, these redundant components would work in active / active mode, so that in addition to failover a uniform load balancing is achieved. However, from the availability perspective, equally important are capacity planning, network monitoring, and an appropriate network design that ensures that all key servers have redundant network interfaces connected to different distribution switches.

Equipment and location of the DR data center. One of the most important decisions in the preparation of DR plan is the choice of location for the disaster recovery center. This decision significantly affects the enforceability of the entire DR plan. It is necessary to take into account that this location is far enough from the primary data center, that they do not share the same risks. On the other hand, it is necessary to consider that it is possible, within the defined RTO, to transfer the DR team to a backup location if needed, and ensure that data replication to the backup location takes place within limits defined by the RPO parameter. This decision should be taken after a thorough evaluation of the risks to which it is exposed the primary data center, as well as risk analysis of potential DR site. Ideally, DR center should be equipped well in order to take a full load from the primary data center. It has to have full-time employees who can immediately start the recovery process in the case of disaster.

Resilient Client/Server systems include technologies, tools, and procedures that maximize system availability in cases when errors occur on the server side. Concepts technologies that are commonly used for this purpose are failover and load balancing clustering, virtualisation and SaaS (software as service) (Marcus & Stern, 2003), (Singh, 2009), (Liu, Deters, & Zhang, 2010), (Calzolari, 2006), (Eric Bauer, 2010), (Bajgoric, 2008). In addition to these concepts, for improving the availability of client-server systems, Liu and colleagues (2010) recommend the use of "explicit messaging, uniform interface, partitioning, self-management and decentralized control "concepts. Cai (2008) presented the idea of proactive self-regulating dynamic optimization of availability based on a dynamic risk assessment

Monitoring by ITIL definition refers to the activity of observing systems for detecting changes that occur during the operation time. It includes the following techniques and tools: tools to monitor the status of key system components and key operations; alerts and warning generation and distribution to responsible employees when defined conditions are met; ensuring that the performance and utilization of components or systems are within a certain range (for example, disk space or memory usage); detection of abnormal types or levels of activity in infrastructure (e.g. a potential security threat); detection of unauthorized changes (e.g. unauthorized software installation); ensuring compliance with the organization's policy (for example, inappropriate use of e-mail); monitoring the service results and ensuring that they meet the quality requirements; monitoring of information used to measure key performance indicators (KPI).

ITIL defines the process control as managing usage or behavior of a component, systems or services. Control requires three conditions: actions must ensure that the behavior is in accordance with the defined standard or norm; circumstances that trigger the action must be defined, clear and confirmed; action must be defined, approved and appropriate for the circumstances.

Human Resources Management is also critical for ensuring IS availability. ITIL framework underscores the value of people in the services management and states that organizations often feel that a simple purchase or developing of the tools will solve all their problems. As the skills necessary for effective and efficient service management, regardless of the role, ITIL recognizes the following: awareness of business priorities and objectives; awareness of the role of IT in enabling business objectives that must be met; the skills needed to provide service to clients; awareness of what IT can provide to a business, including the latest features; competence, knowledge and information they need to successfully meet the given role; the ability to use, understand and interpret the best practices, policies and procedures to ensure their compliance.

MODEL

As noted before, the Leaky Noisy-OR model introduced by Franke et al. (2012) was starting point for this research. In addition to changes in model variables, the elicitation method has been modified as well. According to Diez et al. (2007) there is no much difference between using net or compound parameters during parameters elicitation because the difference is less than an error in expert's subjective estimate. We decided to follow the recommendation and use net parameters, and ask elicitation question according to that decision. Another change of the original model was adding prior probabilities for every causal factor. Since, by definition, BBN use prior probabilities and calculate posterior probabilities based on new information, it was very important to introduce priors into model. If data about priors are not available, one could ask the experts about the state of implementation of the best practices in the field represented by the variable. Answer to that question was used to parameterize prior probabilities for every node. Equation (27) is used for calculating availability:

$$P(A) = (1 - p_0) \prod_{i \in [i,n]} (1 - p_i) = (1 - p_0) \prod_{i \in [i,n]} (1 - kV_i(1 - B_i)) \tag{27}$$

In this formula: n represents the number of variables in the model, V_i - percentage of the improving system's availability if the best practices are applied, B_i – a state of implementation of the best practices in different system's components, k - transformation coefficient, p_0- a leak representing probability that the system is unavailable in the case that for all domains included in the model, best practices are applied.

V_i is obtained as a weighted average of expert answers to the question "How much would be reduced unavailability of IT systems if they were applied best practices the variable domain represented by X?". B_i is obtained as weighted average on the second question "At what level of maturity is particular IS in this area?". These parameters represent the fact that the impact of best practice is not the same if it is already applied on 30% or 90% of existing IS. Equation (27) shows that if the best practices are already

Figure 2. Leaky Noisy-OR BBN model
(Source: Authors' illustration)

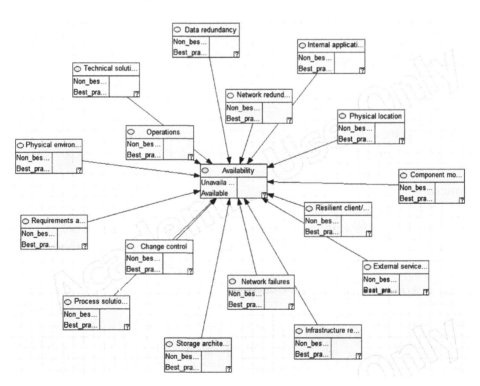

implemented in some domain i.e. state variable Bi = 1, this variable does not affect the availability, or acts like an activated inhibitor. Bi are modeled in the BBN in CPT for nodes representing causal factors. CPT for availability node is filed with values k*Vi for every parent node (causal factors) as it shown in Figure 3.

One of the biggest weaknesses of initial model was lack on economic aspect. To overcome that problem and support investment decision process, the initial BBN model is expanded by adding decision nodes and utility nodes for every causal factor and creating the influence diagram (Figure 4). Expected loss is value modeled as the sum of the losses incurred due to the unavailability of the system and the investment costs to bring particular variable to the level of best practices. Unavailability values below 97% were not modeled because of the assumption, that if an IS of a financial institution is not available 11 days in a year, that organization cannot survive on the market. The formula for calculating the total loss:

$$EL = R \text{ for } A < 97\%$$

$$EL = (1-A)*R + \sum I_i \quad (28)$$

EL: The total expected loss due to unavailability and investment costs.
A: System availability as a percentage.
R: Total loss in the period of 3 years in the case of the total system unavailability.
I_i: Investment needed to bring individual variable to the level of best practices.

Investments required to bring the variables to the level of best practices have been obtained on the basis of the third question that the experts were asked: "What investment (including three-year costs), is needed to take this dimension to the level of best practices?". As an investment depends on organization size, only the experts working in the banks were asked, and their answers were weighted with asset size of the bank they work in. The total loss is a constant that every organization would take from their finan-

Figure 3. Table of conditional probability for a variable availability

Parent	Physical...	Require...	Operations	Change c...	Technica...	Process...	Data red...	Storage...	Infrastruct...	Internal a...	External s...	Network r...	Network f...	Physical I...	Resilient...	Compon...	LEAK
State	Non_best...	Non_best...	Non_best...	Non_best...	Non_best...	Non_best...	Non_best...	Non_best...	Non_best...	Non_best...	Non_best...	Non_best...	Non_best...	Non_best...	Non_best...	Non_best...	
Unavailable	0.072938	0.244904	0.222214	0.273513	0.060196	0.025974	0.069101	0.018564	0.019092	0.160186	0.077372	0.066725	0.1746393	0.023727	0.026754	0.253942	0.01
Available	0.927061	0.755095	0.777785	0.726486	0.939803	0.974025	0.930898	0.981435	0.980907	0.839813	0.922627	0.933274	0.8253607	0.976272	0.973245	0.746057	0.99

cial statements. The model is shown in figure 2. For each node representing causal factors, two more nodes are added. One is a decision node representing dilemma whether to invest in bringing to the variable level of best practices, and the second represents the investment costs ("Utility" node) associated with bringing individual variable level to the level best practice

Each decision node has two choices "Invest" and "Do not invest." Each utility node has two values. If the decision is "Do not invest" value is 0, and in the case that the decision is "Invest" has the value of the investment cost (represented by a negative number as a cost) (Figure 5).

Investment decisions change CPT for the node representing the causal factor variable, so that the probability of best practices is changing to 1 in the case of investments, and if organization choose not to invest, remain on the values obtained from the experts (Bi) (Figure 6).

Figure 4. Influence diagram

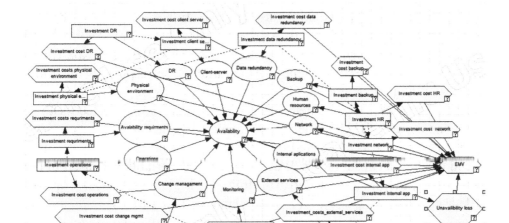

Figure 5. Utility node table for the cost of investing in change management. The value in the table is the model example for the institution of 700 million in assets

Investment change mgmt	Invest	Not_invest
▶ Value	-257513	0

Figure 6. CPT for change management. The values in the table were obtained by elicitation

Investment change mgmt	Invest	Not_invest
NPN	0	0.44355609
▶ NPD	1	0.55644391

Two utility nodes are added to the model: the node that represents the unavailability cost and node that represents total costs (expected loss). The goal of the model is to minimize the expected loss by investing in the implementation of best practices in the domain represented by variables.

The Model Structure Validation

Once the model structure is determined, it was necessary to validate the structure. In order to do that, two approaches were possible: a) structural validation with the experts and b) formal validation according to the rules for the construction of BBN network (Pearl, 1988). As the model presented here is the simplest form of Bayesian networks, validation with experts was reduced to validate the completeness of the variable's set, especially regarding changes of the Franke et al. model. During the interviews, only two experts had an objection to the completeness of the model, deeming it necessary to insert one more variable, while others agreed with the choice of variables.

One of the experts suggested that the model should include the training of end users as a causal factor. We found that this variable was used in the previous research, it was included in the framework that Weill (2002) proposed to determine the infrastructural requirements necessary for the implementation of e-business models. Another expert suggested that the model should include a variable for representing the support of upper management in the process of designing or selection of applications.

Model Parameterization

The probability elicitation used for determining the model parameters was done by interviewing 23 experts dealing with IT systems availability in the financial sector of international banks in Europe. Authors focused on information systems in the banking industry which, due to the presence of international and local regulations and regular audit reviews, have the necessary maturity level of IS governance to be suitable for modeling. During the elicitation, most experts agreed that the selection of variables in the model is adequate and that the model is comprehensive. Elicitation was conducted through structured interviews. In the first part of meetings, experts were trained and calibrated, while in the second part experts filled in the questionnaire. The questionnaire consisted of three sets of questions. Experts were first asked to estimate the impact of individual variables on system availability. In the second question, experts gave their assessment of the situation in the areas described by the variables in the local financial sector. To answer the third question, they estimated the necessary investments to bring the field represented by the variable to the level of best practices. Each question was accompanied by a control question intended to measure a degree of certainty in the answer to the previous question. This question is used to determine the weighting factor for each answer.

Expert Elicitation

The main reason for using expert opinion is the lack of data on the IS "outages" and their causes. Another reason is a need for "linking IS design-science research with practical experience" (March, Hevner, & Ram, 2000)

Selection and Motivation

Before starting the expert selection process, selection criteria should be established, in order to determine the criteria based on which a person is considered an expert. According to Hora (2007) these criteria are:

- Publications and obtained grants in the field of research.
- Works cited.
- Degrees, awards, or other types of recognitions.
- Recommendations and nominations from respectable individuals and professional bodies.
- Positions held.
- Membership or appointments to review boards, commissions, etc.

In addition to these indicators, experts must meet certain additional requirements. The expert should be free of motivational bias caused by economic, political, or other interests in the decision. Experts should be prepared to participate in the process and should be accountable for its assessment. That means they should be prepared to have their names associated with the given answer. Many times, physical proximity, or availability at a particular time, is a major factor in the choice of experts (Hora, 2007).

The main criteria for selection the experts who participated in the study was a good understanding of information system availability issues in the banking sector. Therefore, the population consisted of managers of IT departments of banks (or heads of departments responsible for IT security) and IT auditors who audit the IT systems of international banks. All invited auditors have positively responded and take part in the research (out of 10), and 13 (of 23) invited representatives of banks. Training Even though using expert opinion can resolve the problems of missing data for model parameterization, it introduces different kind of problems like using heurism and biases. Bias is a systematic tendency considering factors that are irrelevant to the task, or to ignore the relevant facts, and thus fails to make a conclusion that at an appropriate normative theory, i.e. probability theory, was classified as essential (Renooij, 2001). There are two types of bias: motivational and cognitive. Motivational biases arise due to expert personal interests and the expert's position in a research context. In the context of this study, motivational bias might arise when experts give their opinion based on the situation in their organizations, which would lead to presenting the situation better than it is, or to demonstrate significant knowledge in the all elicited domains. Cognitive bias occurs when expert's estimates do not follow the normative, statistical or logical rules, because of the way human beings process information (Adusei-Poku, 2005). This type of bias arises from the use of heuristics. It is human nature to simplify the task by using heuristics (rules of thumb) when giving probability estimates (Tversky & Kahneman, 1974). This type of bias is characterized by:

- **Inconsistency:** When an expert becomes inconsequential in thinking. Inconsistency may arise among others due to fatigue while filling in the large table of conditional probabilities (Korb & Nicholson, 2011).
- **Availability:** A type of heuristics in which an expert assesses the likelihood of the event by the ease with which he remembers certain events. The idea behind these heuristics is in fact that the expert will easily remember the events that occur more recently, and therefore, he assigns a high probability to these events. Applying these heuristics often gives adequate results, but also can lead to erroneous estimates of the frequency of certain events.

- **Anchoring:** When an expert starts with the assessment based on the first impression and maintains that estimate with only minor corrections (Adusei-Poku, 2005), (Fox & Clemen, 2005). In the course of this research, an availability bias was the most present.

Experts had a tendency to form probability estimates remembering the events happened recently. That caused the problem of underestimation of high impact – low-frequency events. During the training, it was pointed out the possible biases and heuristics and warned expert on basic techniques of avoiding biases and heuristic with the goal to get better probability estimate. Structuring the Questionnaire Before the interview, the experts who participated in the probability elicitation were introduced with a short description of all variables. In addition, the experts were introduced with the graphical representation of the model and thus further clarified the meaning of the variables.

Elicitation and Documentation

For probability elicitation, direct method was used, where the expert had to choose between one of the offered intervals as his probability assessment.

According to von Winterfeldt and Edwards (1986), elicitation process requires interaction between one or preferably two elicitors and one or more experts. Elicitor has several tasks:

- He has to help an expert in the problems that inevitably arise in the interpretation of questions, definitions of variables and values, and so on.
- Elicitor should record all information expressed by experts, even they cannot be recorded in a prescribed questionnaire, but still can be useful. For example, information on variables that are not included in the research or variables that are not relevant to a given decision according to expert's opinion. Also, if the expert overestimated the probability of a particular distribution of conditional probabilities so that their sum exceeds 100% it is possible to make an adjustment during elicitation.
- It could happen that certain contexts, for which probability assessment is asked, are incomplete or unnecessary. For probabilistic networks, this means that the network structure should be changed, and therefore, it is important that this information is carefully recorded.
- Elicitor could expect that expert introduces biases in answering to some questions and during elicitation, he should warn experts to possible biases.

- Elicitor needs to look at the clock: the elicitation is harder for experts than for elicitor and, therefore, the duration of the session should not exceed one hour.

Despite these tasks, elicitor should avoid taking too much control and guidance on concrete answers. The expert should be relaxed, without feeling that his attitude challenged because he is an expert whose opinion is valued (Cooke, 1991).

According to the above recommendations, elicitation was performed in one-hour meetings with the experts. The experts were asked to fill out a questionnaire in predefined Google sheets. During the elicitation process in over half cases, the experts needed help to understand correctly the meaning of the variables and understand question's response format, to avoid biases, especially availability bias. The experts were often tempted to define the probability remembering the last events that had a negative impact on availability.

Verification

After elicitation, data verification was carried out. Verification is the process of checking whether the probability obtained from experts is well-calibrated (if they are in accordance with the observed frequencies), that you obey the laws of probability (to be coherent) and reliable.

Checking whether the estimates are consistent it is often impossible because the events for which the estimated probability often cannot be seen or otherwise measured. As for coherence, it is possible to check whether the sum of all assessed probabilities equals to one.

Test-retest reliability checks if the experts agree with his assessment that is, whether it will provide the same expert assessment when asked again for the same probability. However, in the case of probabilistic networks, the number of elicitated parameters is likely to be so large, that it is impossible to assess it more than once. Instead of testing the reliability of using a separate assessment, the expert may be given an option to evaluate the entire probability distribution that occurred in the elicitation. An indication of the validity of the assessment may also be obtained by filling CPT of the probabilistic network and calculating the effect of the observations on probabilities for some variables of interest. Results for these variables can then be checked against the available data or be presented to experts (Renooij, 2001). This method was used, and the research results were sent to ten experts for evaluation. Eight answers were received without any major objection to the research results.

RESULTS

The results show that the variables with the greatest influence on EMV maximization are "requirements on availability" and "operations management," i.e. minimal investment to bring these fields to the best practices level would significantly benefit in improving IS availability. On the other side, results show that the relationship between investment and the effect on the availability is the lowest in the field of physical environment and client-server solutions. The biggest investment for bringing the field to the best practices level are needed for variable DR location and equipment, which also has a major impact on availability.

Figure 7 shows the possible combinations of investments obtained as a result of solving influence diagram. Each point shown in the diagram represents one value of the investment function (which includes the sum of investment to a certain set of variables Xp to the level of best practices and loss as a result of unavailability) and related IS availability value. It is evident that by choosing different investment strategies, for the same level of invested funds organization can achieve a different availability level. The optimal level of investment for each level of availability is achieved by selecting a combination of investments that are on the lower edge of the diagram. In the analysed case the bank with 700 million in assets, the assumed loss of 190.26 $ per minute unavailability and other parameters obtained elicitation, solution

Figure 7. The set of investment decision to achieve desired availability level (Source: Author's Illustration)

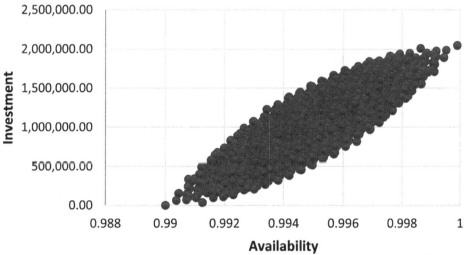

of the influence diagrams, which minimizes the impact of the expected loss is a combination of investment in bringing the "management request on availability" and "management operations" the level of best practices. This solution reduces the total loss of 999,752.07 (the level of availability of 99%) to 905443.38 (99.229% level of availability and investment of -135364.46 $).

From practical point of view every organization can produce similar graph following these steps:

Identify All Relevant Systems and Services and Determine their Current Availability Level

System availability can be calculated based on recorded incidents and planned events that caused the system unavailability in the previous period. If, during this period there were not recorded low frequency -high impact events, then it is necessary to make an additional adjustment of the availability level. Transformation coefficient- the required for the model parameterization can be obtained based on the current value of system availability. Table 1 represents recorded availability of the system components with service weight, measuring relative service importance.

Measure States of Individual Variables

States of individual variables (B_i) could be taken based on the findings of the external or internal audit of IT systems. IT audit is usually conducted according COBIT and is expressed as a maturity level for each reviewed area. Results of external audit cannot be taken as a deterministic, due to non-

Table 1. Recorded availability of the system components

Subsystem	Planned (Hours)	Unplanned (Hours)	SLA	Service Availability	Service Weight
ERP	24	20	24*7	99.49634%	1
CRM	12	30	24*7	99.51923%	0.7
General ledger	12	5	5*10	99.34615%	0.5
Payroll	32	20	24*7	99.40476%	0.2
POS	36	36	24*7	99.17582%	0.7
MRP	8	15	6*10	99.26282%	0.7
Sales order	16	25	24*7	99.53068%	0.7

negligible possibility of error in the preparation of the audit findings. Based on results of this research, it can be assumed that audit findings behave per the rules of normal distribution, with mean based around audit appraisal. Table 2 presents the state of the system for all included domains/variables.

Calculate Potential Unavailability Loss

Unavailability loss can be determined by calculating the following factors:

- Loss of income of unrealized services, obtained as the average revenue from services per hour.

Table 2. Audit appraisal for each variable

Domain/variable	Description	Grade/Subsystems Average
Physical environment	Server room with basic equipment	7
Availability requirements management	Basic requirements collection often unstructured	5
Operations management	There is SIEM system for collecting, monitoring and reporting of all significant system logs	7
Change management	There are prescribed procedures, often violated	6
Backup management	There is a set process of tape back	8
Storage redundancy	There are RAID systems on all key servers, asynchronous replication to the DR site with RPO at 5 minutes	7
Avoiding errors in internal applications	Stable application that allows seamless provision of customer service, problems in the implementation of the new version	7
Avoiding errors in external services	Most of the service is dependent on a single service provider	5
Network management	Network infrastructure set up with redundant components and cold backup replacement devices	8
Equipment and location of the (DR) data center	There is a DR data center equipped with basic equipment to continue operating. Critical data are replicated from the primary data center	8
Resilient client/server systems	All essential services are Active / Active and Active / Passive x86 clusters	7
Monitoring of relevant components	There is implemented a monitoring system with e-mail notifications	7
Human resources management	There are rewarding and education plans, partialy executed	6

- Loss of income from productivity, obtained as the average labor expenditure per hour.
- The loss incurred in the of service recovery process.
- Loss of income from clients who have left the firm because of the system unavailability o.
- Loss of income from clients who did not come to the firm because of the system unavailability.

Suppose that the organization has a total annual income 50 million USD, of which 23 million USD are service revenues. The potential losses in a longer period may be significantly higher than the annual income of the organization, due to loss of customers, current and potential (arising from the inability to provide service and reputation risk), caused by the system unavailability. In extreme cases, when the availability drops below the level of e.g. 95% percent of the firm may go into bankruptcy. Those facts should be taken in consideration when modeling unavailability loss.

Assessing Potential Investment to Bring Variable to the Best Practices Level

Deepening on states of every variable assessed in step two, size of organization, current technology level, and potential investment value can be calculated. As a starting point for looking for the best practices in every domain, an organization can use COBIT, ITIL or results of this research which combine multiple sources, academic as well as various industry standards and practices (Ibrahimovic, 2015).

Once an organization has results from all previous steps it is easy to get optimal investment solution, constrained with available budget, using proposed model.

REAL WORLD CASES

Bank Ensures High Availability, Promotes Business Growth, and Boosts Performance with New Database Solution, Ensures High Uptime for Critical Customer-Facing Applications

One of Brazil's largest banks, Banco Bradesco, has more than 65 million customers throughout the country. Many of these customers depend on the bank's online banking and customer service applications. To make sure these mission-critical applications are available around the clock, the bank is implementing a Microsoft high-availability and disaster-recovery solution based on Microsoft SQL Server 2012. With that high availability ensured, the bank can provide better customer service. The solution will also help support the bank's growth, and it improves performance by up to 30 percent. Banco Bradesco now has a solution that ensures high availability for its critical applications. In addition, the new Microsoft solution has improved the bank's customer service and boosted performance by 30 percent. The bank also expects the solution to lead to increased business. With SQL Server 2012, Banco Bradesco can provide high availability for its critical customer-facing SharePoint Server portal. "Our tests showed that SQL Server 2012 will give us much higher availability, and we will definitely decrease downtime for our customer applications," says Okamato. "This improvement will positively affect our customers, because they rely on our applications to always be available to them." Available at: https://www.microsoft.com/danmark/cases/Microsoft-SQL-Server-2012-Enterprise/Banco-Bradesco/Bank-Ensures-High-Availability-Promotes-Business-Growth-and-Boosts-Performance-with-New-Database-Solution/710000000969

Company: One of the US Top Five Banks, Serving Millions of Consumer and Business Customers in Over 50 Countries.

How one of the world's largest banks ensures 24x7 business continuity and service availability. With millions of customers accessing the bank systems daily at ATMs, branches, online, and through multiple call centers, any downtime or service disruptions are practically unacceptable to the bank. With a growing portion of customers relying on online and mobile banking, 24/7 service reliability has become more critical than ever. To address these needs, major efforts and resources have been directed towards the creation of a robust high availability and disaster recovery infrastructure. In this complex infrastructure comprising multiple datacenters, configuration changes are undertaken daily by different groups in various parts of the environment. While each team was making an effort to apply best practices in its own domain, there was no visibility to the implications and risks introduced by such modifications on the overall stability, service availability, and DR readiness of critical systems. Available at: http://www.continuitysoftware.com/wp-content/uploads/2013/07/Banking-Case-Study.pdf

Bank of Israel: Addressing Disaster Recovery and High Availability Challenges with Continuity Software

This case study looks at Bank of Israel's (BOI) disaster recovery (DR) and high availability challenges surrounding the need to protect and ensure the continuous availability and performance of its critical data center operations. The study analyzes the benefits gained by BOI by implementing Continuity Software's solutions, which are aimed at allowing organizations to continuously assess their DR readiness, avoid system downtime, data loss or data corruption, as well as ensuring regulatory compliance. Available at: http://www.continuitysoftware.com/wp-content/uploads/2013/04/Bank-of-Israel_-Addressing-DR-and-HA-Challenges-with-Continuity-Software_0_0.pdf

The Business Challenge: Civista Bank

High availability is critical for financial institutions; however, legacy backup tools can get in the way. That was the case for Civista Bank until it replaced its legacy backup tool with Veeam® Backup Essentials™, a decision that set in motion a sophisticated, cyclical backup and replication strategy for disaster recovery (DR) and business continuity. The legacy backup tool had only performed full backups. They were so time-consuming that only the most critical VMs could be backed up weekly, leaving the remaining VMs to be backed up monthly. The limited number of recovery points had taken a toll on the IT team's ability to deliver high availability. Civista Bank didn't stop there. To further enhance high availability, the bank replaced another legacy system. "Our storage had reached its end of life, and its performance capabilities were dated," said Neal D. Barrett, Network Administrator at Civista Bank. "We wanted to take advantage of storage snapshot technology, but only if we could continue using Veeam. We had placed our trust in Veeam for DR and business resumption, and Veeam had proven itself year after year. Trust is not something I place in many IT products and services, but I've used several generations of Veeam, and it has earned my trust. The key differentiator that drove our storage choice wasn't performance, features, scalability, purchase price or even total cost of ownership. The key differentiator was integration with Veeam." Available at: https://www.veeam.com/success-stories/bank-invests-in-high-availability-with-veeam-netapp-and-cisco.html

CHAPTER SUMMARY

In this chapter, we explained steps taken in the model building process and introduced a formula for measuring availability of complex systems. The selection of independent variables with a definition of each of the variables in the model is described in more details (best practices in the field). Independent variables included in the model are: the physical environment, availability requirements management, operations management, change management, backup management, storage redundancy, avoiding errors and internal applications, avoiding errors and external services, network management, equipment and location of the DR data centers, resilient client / server systems, monitoring of relevant components, human resources management. Analytical and graphical form of the model were also presented in this chapter. In the further course of the chapter the influence diagram was presented, as an extension of the BBN model from an economic perspective, by including utility and decision nodes into the model. The utility function, which has been used in the model is a linear function that represents the total loss due to the unavailability of the system and investments costs necessary to bring variables to the level of best practices. Increasing investment reduces the loss due to unavailability. The goal of the model was to maximize the expected utility, with the restrictions imposed by the desired level of availability. In the last part of the chapter we explained steps taken during the model parametrization and described BBN model parameterization process using an expert elicitation, from theoretical and practical aspects. Finally, the chapter presents the results of running the model by using Genie 2.0 BBN software and gives by the steps to be taken for application of the model in practice.

REFERENCES

Adusei-Poku, K. (2005). Operational risk management–implementing a Bayesian network for foreign exchange and money market settlement. University of Goettingen.

Bajgoric, N. (2008). *Continuous Computing Technologies for Enhancing Business Continuity*. IGI Global.

Bauer, E. (2010). *Design for Reliability: Information and Computer-Based Systems*. Joh Wiley & Sons, Inc. doi:10.1002/9781118075104

Bonafede, E. C., Cerchiello, P., & Giudici, P. (2007). Statistical models for business continuity management. *Journal of Operational Risk*, *2*(4), 79–96. doi:10.21314/JOP.2007.037

Cai, Z. (2008). *Risk-based proactive availability management-attaining high performance and resilience with dynamic self-management in Enterprise Distributed Systems* [Doctoral dissertation]. Georgia Institute of Technology.

Calzolari, F. (2006). *High availability using virtualization.* Universita di Pisa.

Castagna, R. (2013). *Business backup trends: Storage Purchasing Intentions fall 2012 survey results.* Storage Magazine.

Cemerlic, A., Yang, L., & Kizza, J. M. (2008, July). *Network Intrusion Detection Based on Bayesian Networks* (pp. 791–794). SEKE.

Conradi, H., & Fuggetta, A. (2002). Improving software process improvement. *IEEE Software*, *19*(4), 92–99. doi:10.1109/MS.2002.1020295

Dejaeger, K., & Verbraken, T. (2012). Towards comprehensible software fault prediction models using Bayesian network classifiers (forthcoming). *Transactions on Software*, *1*(1), 1–22.

Diez, F. J., & Druzdzel, M. J. (2006). *Canonical probabilistic models for knowledge engineering* (Technical Report CISIAD-06-01). UNED, Madrid, Spain.

Doguc, O. (2010). *Applications of Bayesian networks in complex system reliability.* Stevens Institute of Technology.

Fenton, N. (2012). *Risk Assessment and Decision Analysis with Bayesian Networks.* CRC Press.

Fenton, N., Hearty, P., Neil, M., & Radliński, Ł. (2010). Software project and quality modelling using Bayesian networks. *Artificial intelligence applications for improved software engineering development: New prospects.*

Fenton, N., Krause, P., & Neil, M. (2001). A probabilistic model for software defect prediction. *IEEE Transactions Software Engineering*, *44*(0), 1–35.

Fenton, N., Marsh, W., Neil, M., Cates, P., Forey, S., & Tailor, M. (2004). Making resource decisions for software projects. *Proceedings of the 26th International Conference on Software Engineering* (pp. 397–406). doi:10.1109/ICSE.2004.1317462

Fenton, N., & Neil, M. (2001). Making decisions: Using Bayesian nets and MCDA. *Knowledge-Based Systems, 14*(7), 307–325. doi:10.1016/S0950-7051(00)00071-X

Fenton, N., & Neil, M. (2007). Managing Risk in the Modern World. In *Application of Bayesian Networks.*

Fineman, M. (2010). *Improved Risk Analysis for Large Projects : Bayesian Networks Approach.* Queen Mary, Unversity of London.

Foroughi, F. (2008, July). Information security risk assessment by using bayesian learning technique.*Proceedings of the World Congress on Engineering* (Vol. 1, p. 133).

Franke, U., Johnson, P., & König, J. (2014). An architecture framework for enterprise IT service availability analysis. *Software {&} Systems Modeling, 13*(4), 1417–1445.

Franke, U., Johnson, P., König, J., & Marcks von Würtemberg, L. (2012). Availability of enterprise IT systems: An expert-based Bayesian framework. *Software Quality Journal, 20*(2), 369–394. doi:10.1007/s11219-011-9141-z

Gnanasundaram, S., & Shrivastava, A. (Eds.), (2012). Information Storage and Management (2nd ed.). Joh Wiley & Sons, Inc.

Gran, B. (2002). Use of Bayesian Belief Networks when combining disparate sources of information in the safety assessment of software-based systems. *International Journal of Systems Science, 33*(6), 529–542. doi:10.1080/00207720210133589

Heckerman, D., Breese, J. S., & Rommelse, K. (1995). Decision-theoretic troubleshooting. *Communications of the ACM, 38*(3), 49–57. doi:10.1145/203330.203341

Hinz, D. J., & Malinowski, J. (2006, January). Assessing the Risks of IT Infrastructure—A Personal Network Perspective. In *Proceedings of the 39th Annual Hawaii International Conference on System Sciences, 2006. HICSS'06.* (Vol. 8, pp. 172a-172a). IEEE.

Houmb, S. H., Georg, G., France, R., Bieman, J., & Jurjens, J. (2005, June). Cost-benefit trade-off analysis using BBN for aspect-oriented risk-driven development. *Proceedings of the 10th IEEE International Conference on Engineering of Complex Computer Systems ICECCS '05* (pp. 195-204). IEEE. doi:10.1109/ICECCS.2005.30

Ibrahimovic, S. (2015). Optimizacija ulaganja u raspoloživost it infrastrukture korištenjem Bayesian Belief Networks model.

Ibrahimovic, S., & Bajgoric, N. (2016). Modeling Information System Availability by Using Bayesian Belief Network Approach. *Interdisciplinary Description of Complex Systems*, *14*(2), 125–138. doi:10.7906/indecs.14.2.2

Johnson, P., Lagerström, R., Narman, P., & Simonsson, M. (2007). Enterprise architecture analysis with extended influence diagrams. *Information Systems Frontiers*, *9*(2-3), 163–180. doi:10.1007/s10796-007-9030-y

Kondakci, S. (2010, August). Network security risk assessment using Bayesian belief networks. *Proceedings of the 2010 IEEE Second International Conference on Social Computing (SocialCom)* (pp. 952-960). IEEE. doi:10.1109/SocialCom.2010.141

Lagerström, R., Johnson, P., Höök, D., & König, J. (2009). Software Change Project Cost Estimation–A Bayesian Network and a Method for Expert Elicitation. *Proceedings of theInternational Workshop on Software Quality and Maintainability*.

Lande, L., S., Zuo, Y., & Pimple, M. (2010, June). A Survivability Decision Model for Critical Information Systems Based on Bayesian Network. *Proceedings of the5th Annual Symposium on Information Assurance (ASIA'10)*.

Linnes, C. (2006). *Applying Decision Theory to Quantify the Cost of Network Security Risk*. Nova Southeastern University.

Liu, D., Deters, R., & Zhang, W. J. (2010). Architectural design for resilience. *Enterprise Information Systems*, *4*(2), 137–152. doi:10.1080/17517570903067751

Marcus, E., & Stern, H. (2003). *Blueprints for high availability* (2nd ed.). Indianapolis, IN, USA: John Wiley & Sons, Inc.

Mendel, T., & Ostergaard, B. (2004, August). A big step toward automating network management. *Forrester*.

Neil, M., Häger, D., & Andersen, L. (2009). Modelling Operational Risk in Financial Institutions using Hybrid Dynamic Bayesian Networks. *Journal of Operational Risk*.

Neil, M., Marquez, D., & Fenton, N. (2008). Using Bayesian networks to model the operational risk to information technology infrastructure in financial institutions. *Journal of Financial Transformation*, *22*, 131–138.

Okutan, A., & Yıldız, O. T. (2012). Software defect prediction using Bayesian networks. *Empirical Software Engineering*, 2.

Raderius, J., Närman, P., & Ekstedt, M. (2008, December). Assessing system availability using an enterprise architecture analysis approach. *Proceedings of theInternational Conference on Service-Oriented Computing* (pp. 351-362). Springer.

Radliński, Ł., Fenton, N., & Neil, M. (2007). Improved decision-making for software managers using Bayesian networks. In *Software Engineering and Applications* (pp. 1–13). SEA.

Rauscher, K. F., Krock, R. E., & Runyon, J. P. (2006). Eight ingredients of communications infrastructure: A systematic and comprehensive framework for enhancing network reliability and security. *Bell Labs Technical Journal, 11*(3), 73–81. doi:10.1002/bltj.20179

Renooij, S. (2001). *Qualitative Approaches to Quantifying Probabilistic Networks*. Universiteit Utrecht.

Roshandel, R., Medvidovic, N., & Golubchik, L. (2007). A Bayesian model for predicting reliability of software systems at the architectural level. *Software Architectures, Components, and Applications. Lecture Notes in Computer Science, 4880*, 108–126. doi:10.1007/978-3-540-77619-2_7

Scott, D. (2005). *Disaster Recovery and Data Replication Architectures*. *Gartner IT Security Summit 2005*.

Simonsson, M., Lagerström, R., & Johnson, P. (2008, August). A Bayesian network for IT governance performance prediction.*Proceedings of the 10th international conference on Electronic commerce*. ACM. doi:10.1145/1409540.1409542

Singh, J. (2009). Modeling application availability.*Proceedings of the 2009 Spring Simulation Multiconference* (pp. 1–4).

Sommestad, T., & Ekstedt, M. (2009). Cyber security risks assessment with Bayesian defense graphs and architectural models. *System Sciences*.

Taylor, S., Cannon, D., & Wheldon, D. (2007). *ITIL Service Operation*. Office of Goverment Commerce.

Taylor, S., Lacy, S., & MacFarlane, I. (2007). *ITIL Service Transition*. London: The Stationary Office.

Taylor, S., Vernon, L., & Rudd, C. (2007). *ITIL Service Design*. London: The Stationary Office.

Wang, C., & Mosleh, A. (2010). Qualitative-Quantitative Bayesian Belief Networks for reliability and risk assessment. *2010 Proceedings - Annual Reliability and Maintainability Symposium (RAMS)*, 1–5.

Weber, P., Medina-Oliva, G., Simon, C., & Iung, B. (2012). Overview on Bayesian networks applications for dependability, risk analysis and maintenance areas. *Engineering Applications of Artificial Intelligence*, 25(4), 671–682. doi:10.1016/j.engappai.2010.06.002

Weber, P., & Suhner, M. (2001). System architecture design based on a Bayesian Networks method. *Proceedings of the 10th International Symposium on Applied Stochastic Models and Data Analysis*, Compiègne, France.

Wei, W., Wang, H., Yang, B., & Liu, L. (2011). A Bayesian Network Based Knowledge Engineering Framework for IT Service Management. *IEEE Transactions on Services Computing*, 99, 1–14.

Yoon, Y. (2003). *Modelling Operational Risk in Financial Institutions using Bayesian Networks*. Cass Business School.

Yu, Y., Zheng, G., & Qian, Z. (2009, November). Software Reliability Model Analysis Including Internal Structure Based on Bayesian Network. *Proceedings of the Fourth International Conference on Cooperation and Promotion of Information Resources in Science and Technology COINFO'09* (pp. 247-251). IEEE. doi:10.1109/COINFO.2009.82

Zhang, R., Cope, E., Heusler, L., & Cheng, F. (2009, October). A Bayesian network approach to modeling IT service availability using system logs. *Proceedings of the Workshop on the analysis of system logs*.

Chapter 6
Model Validation by Using Monte–Carlo Simulation

One of the biggest disadvantages of the proposed model based on influence diagrams is deterministic nature of input parameters. Each parameter in the network is set on the basis of the weighted mean of values obtained in the process of elicitation, not reflecting the diversity of experts' opinion. For this reason, the same mathematical model was implemented using Microsoft Excel and Oracle Crystal Ball software. The base values of the input variables are set in the same way as the parameters of the influence diagram, however, for each input parameter is defined as a random variable. That means each variable is represented not only by the mean value but also using entire distribution obtained in the elicitation process. Figures 1, 2, and 3 show distributions for all three input variables related to the change management.

Using described methodology, the stochastic equivalent of the influence diagram was made. The main goal of this modeling approach is running Monte-Carlo simulations. The first simulation was run without optimization, just applying the distribution obtained by elicitation. Each simulation has had a total of 10 000 trials and some of the results are shown in Figures 4, 5 and 6.

The graphs, presented on the Figures 3, 4, 5 and 6 show the stochastic nature of availability prediction. If there are 13 variables, which can affect the availability and which are not at the best practices level, it is not possible

DOI: 10.4018/978-1-5225-2268-3.ch006

Figure 1. Probability distribution of investments cost in the change management
Source: Author's Illustration

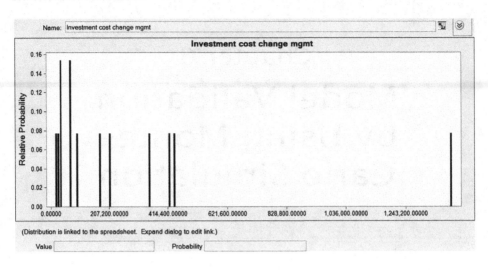

Figure 2. Probability distribution for the state of the change management
Source: Author's Illustration

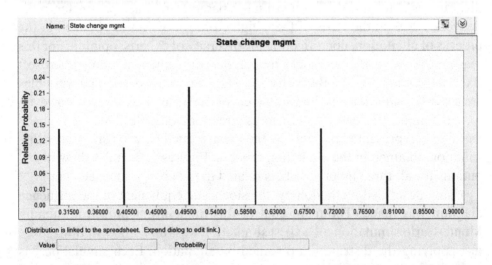

to precisely determine the time and the effect that this weakness may cause. Thus, it is not possible accurately to predict the IS availability percentage, rather, it is possible to predict that availability will be inside the predicted range with particular certainty level. According to the results of the simulation, authors got the IS availability range from 98.33% to 99.76% with 90% confidence for the case in which best practice are not applied. Mean and

Model Validation by Using Monte-Carlo Simulation

Figure 3. Probability distribution for the impact of the change management
Source: Author's Illustration

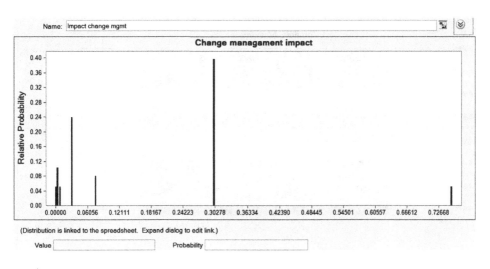

Figure 4. Probability distribution for IS availability after running Monte- Carlo simulation
Source: Author's Illustration

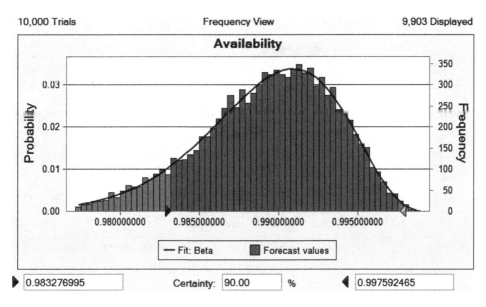

Figure 5. IS availability certainty intervals
Source: Author's Illustration

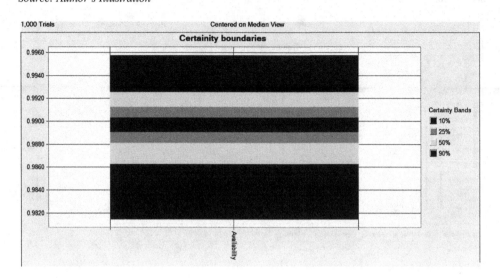

Figure 6. Probability distribution for IS unavailability loss
Source: Author's Illustration

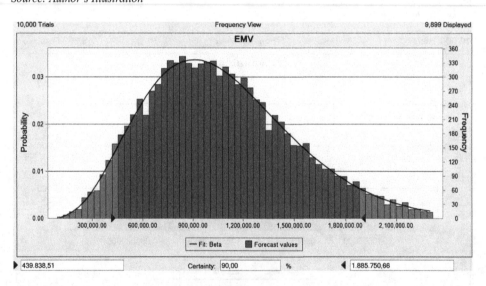

median values were 98.93% and 98.97% respectively, which was close to the initial assumption of 99%.

Data losses linearly correspond to the availability data. The justification for this approximation can be derived from the fact that in the range from 99% to 99.99%, which was modeled, lost curve is almost linear. Figure 7

Figure 7. Unavailability cost function r(A)=k*1/A100
Source: Author's Illustration

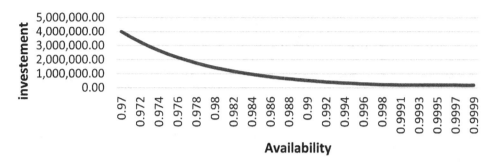

shows an example of a cost function using the formula with high non-linearity, but despite that, in the analyzed range, it is approaching a linear function. In the example, the uncertainty in the losses amount was modeled using a normal distribution with a mean of $100,000,000 and a standard deviation of $10,000,000. Simulation results, using default parameter values, predicts a total loss in range 439,838.51 and 1,885,750.66 with the certainty of 90 with a mean value of 1,072,845.82 and a median value equals 1,023,797.13, which approximately corresponds to the initial assumption of 999,752.07.

An optimization using the Crystal Ball software had also been made. This optimization is working on a basis of thousands (in our case 10 000) various "what if" cases, changing the values of input variables according to their distributions, as well as decision values. All the inputs and results for each calculation was saved as a scenario. Scenarios analysis provided decision recommendation optimizing the EMV for minimizing mean of total loss. The results of this analysis are shown in the following table (Table 1).

These findings are partially different from optimization results obtained by solving influence diagram. However, differences are minor and can be attributed stochastically nature of the Monte-Carlo simulation with respect to the deterministic character of the BBN network parameters. It can be noticed that the same solution is in second place in both methods, with a less than 0.3% difference comparing to the best solution according to the of minimizing the EMV criteria. However, at the same time, using this solution, with minor costs increase organization can achieve a significant increase in availability. Thus, the sensitivity analysis shows that the deterministic version is relatively robust.

The Crystal Ball software was used for the designing optimal investment strategies to achieve availability goal according to organization's risk appetite. Crystal Ball has a particular function for an efficient frontier construction

Table 1. Crystal ball simulation results

Rank	EMV	Investment client server	investment DR	Investment external services	Investment internal app	Investment HR	Investment monitoring	Investment backup	Investment physical environment	Investment operation	Investment data redundancy	Investment change mgmt	Investment availability requirements	Investment network
1	958,134.17	0	0	0	0	0	1	0	0	0	0	0	1	0
2	961,066.97	0	0	0	0	0	1	0	0	1	0	0	1	0
3	981,987.46	0	0	0	0	0	1	1	0	0	0	0	1	0
4	984,881.50	0	0	0	0	0	1	1	0	1	0	0	1	0
5	987,749.32	0	0	0	0	0	1	0	0	0	0	1	1	0
6	990,593.94	0	0	0	0	0	1	0	0	1	0	1	1	0
7	992,634.16	0	0	0	0	0	0	0	0	0	0	0	1	0
8	995,685.71	0	0	0	0	0	0	0	0	1	0	0	1	0

(Source: Author's Illustration)

based on the modern portfolio theory (Markowitz, 1952). Modern portfolio theory has a goal to find optimal investment strategy to maximize profit and at the same time minimize variability (standard deviation) thereby construct a curve of efficient solutions that minimize risk for each desired level of profit. In this study, the efficient frontier was used, with the goal to minimize total cost (EMV), for every availability value from 99% to 99.99% with step 0.0001. For each step, Crystal Ball made 1000 "what if" analysis and for every availability, the value found the optimal investments to bring domains represented by the variables to the best practices level. Using this procedure, the efficient frontier curve shown was produced (Figure 8).

DISCUSSION

According to the results of this research, the perception of experts is that the state of the essential IS infrastructure elements, including the server room, server and network infrastructure, data redundancy, backup management is much better than the process part, which includes change management, operations management, monitoring and requirements management. Assess-

Figure 8. Efficient frontier
Source: Author's Illustration

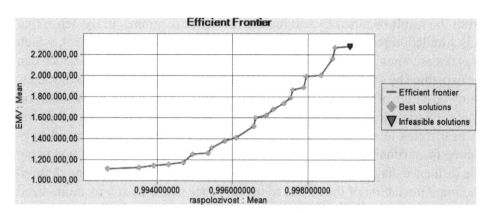

ment of the current maturity level of backup management may explain why the experts estimated that implementing best practices in that area would have a small impact on reducing unavailability, as the situation in that field has been assessed as the best compared to all other areas that were part of the model. A similar explanation applies to the physical environment and server infrastructure.

The model is aimed at maximizing the expected utility, with the restrictions imposed by the desired level of availability. When tried to solve the model without limit imposed to the availability level, the optimal level of investment was very low (in this case only investment in requirements management and monitoring). Main reasons were: relatively high (99%) initial level of IS availability and diminishing return for investments made to raise availability level above 99.5%. On the other hand, there are regulations on the IS management, which impose the application of best practice in specific areas represented in the model. Another reason for investing could be the risk avoidance attitude adopted by a bank management. Those two reasons could be the driving force for investing above the optimal level.

Although the utility function does not have the maximum value, if an investment has been made to achieve the best practice level in the IS monitoring and control area, one-dimensional tornado analysis has shown that investment in that area should be made. The main reason for investing is that 25% percentage variation in the dependent variable can be eliminated if best practice level in that field is achieved. The influence diagram has been validated using the Monte-Carlo analysis in which each variable takes values from the distribution emerged from the elicitation, instead of using average values as in the influence diagram.

The value of that simulation is that it takes into account the stochastic nature of the causes of IS unavailability. The optimization result is partially different from the result obtained by solving the influence diagrams, in the sense that this simulation recommends investment in IS monitoring and control, which was not recommended by solving the influence diagram. This difference can be explained by the stochastic character of this model, as opposed to the deterministic nature of the influence diagram. In addition, Monte-Carlo simulation was used to make the analysis of optimal levels of investment for achieving IS availability levels between 99% to 99.9% in steps of 0.01%. The results obtained from running this simulation correspond to the results obtained using the influence diagram. An external validation of the model was done through the implementation of the model to one instance of the IS at a medium-sized international banks. The starting point availability level was 99.381%, and losses due to the unavailability were $619,490 per year. The solution of the model for the particular case showed that the optimal solution is to invest in availability requirements management and IS monitoring and control. The resulting availability was 99.492%, and the sum of investment costs and the costs of the loss, caused by unavailability were $603,854. When the minimum availability parameter was set to 99.9%, the results changed and implied investment in all areas except in disaster recovery location and human resources. The sum of investment cost and the cost due to unavailability was $1,457,175.87.

REAL WORLD CASES: SOFTWARE PACKAGES

GeNIe Modeler

GeNIe Modeler is a graphical user interface (GUI) to SMILE Engine and allows for interactive model building and learning. It is written for the Windows environment but can be also used on Mac OS and Linux under Windows emulators. It has been thoroughly tested in the field since 1998, has received a wide acceptance within both academia and industry, and has thousands of users world-wide. An important design criterion for all our products has been from the very start that they should allow for a complete modeling freedom. GeNIe models do not bend reality to available modeling tools. Whatever the domain demands, can be modeled in our software. Because no exact algorithms exist for some type of models, our software is equipped with a suite of approximate stochastic sampling algorithms, capable of solving any models created by the users. Available at: http://www.bayesfusion.com/genie-modelerhttps://dslpitt.org/dsl/

Oracle: Crystal Ball

Oracle Crystal Ball is the leading spreadsheet-based application for predictive modeling, forecasting, simulation, and optimization. It gives you unparalleled insight into the critical factors affecting risk. With Crystal Ball, you can make the right tactical decisions to reach your objectives and gain a competitive edge under even the most uncertain market conditions.

- Builds on existing Monte Carlo and predictive modeling tools.
- Provides advanced optimization and calculation capabilities.
- Combines Oracle Crystal Ball and Oracle Crystal Ball Decision Optimizer.

Available at: http://www.oracle.com/us/products/applications/crystalball/overview/index.html

Palisade: The Decision Tools, Palisade

Wouldn't you like to know the chances of making money on your next venture? Or which of many decision options is most likely to yield the best payoff? How about the best sequential drilling strategy? Or how much to invest in various projects in order to maximize the return on your project portfolio? Everyone would like answers to these types of questions. Armed with that kind of information, you could take a lot of guesswork out of big decisions and plan strategies with confidence. With the DecisionTools Suite, you can answer these questions and more – right in your Excel spreadsheet. The DecisionTools Suite is an integrated set of programs for risk analysis and decision making under uncertainty that runs in Microsoft Excel. The DecisionTools Suite includes @RISK, which adds risk analysis to Excel using Monte Carlo simulation, PrecisonTree for visual decision tree analysis, TopRank for what-if analysis, NeuralTools and StatTools for data analysis, and RISKOptimizer and Evolver for optimization. Rounding out the Suite is BigPicture for mind mapping, diagramming, and data exploration. Available at: http://www.palisade.com/decisiontools_suite/

Netica Application, Norsys Software

Netica is a powerful, easy-to-use, complete program for working with belief networks and influence diagrams. It has an intuitive and smooth user interface for drawing the networks, and the relationships between variables may be entered as individual probabilities, in the form of equations, or learned from data files (which may be in ordinary tab-delimited form and have "missing data"). Once a network is created, the knowledge it contains can be transferred to other networks by cutting and pasting, or saved in modular form by creating a library of nodes with disconnected links. Of course, the networks and libraries may be saved in files or printed out. Netica can use the networks to perform various kinds of inference using the fastest and most modern algorithms. Given a new case of which we have limited knowledge, Netica will find the appropriate values or probabilities for all the unknown variables. These values or probabilities may be displayed in a number of different ways, including bar graphs and meters. The case may conveniently be saved to a file, and later brought back into the network (or a different network) for further querying, or to take into account new information about the case. Netica can use influence diagrams to find optimal decisions which maximize the expected values of specified variables. Netica can construct conditional plans, since decisions in the future can depend on observations yet to be made, and the timings and inter-relationships between decisions are considered. Available at: http://www.norsys.com/netica.html

Free and Open Source Bayesian Network Software

- **Banjo (Bayesian Network Inference with Java Objects):** Static and dynamic Bayesian networks.
- Bayesian Network Tools in Java (BNJ) for research and development using graphical models of probability. It is implemented in 100% pure Java.
- **BUGS:** Bayesian Inference using Gibbs Sampling – Bayesian analysis of complex statistical models using Markov chain Monte Carlo methods.
- **Dlib C++ Library:** With extensive Bayesian Network support.
- Dynamic Bayesian Network Simulator.
- **FBN:** Free Bayesian Network for constraint based learning of Bayesian networks.
- JavaBayes is a system that calculates marginal probabilities and expectations, produces explanations, performs robustness analysis, and allows the user to import, create, modify and export networks.
- jBNC is a Java toolkit for training, testing, and applying Bayesian Network Classifiers.
- JNCC2 is the Java implementation of the Naive Credal Classifier 2.

- MSBNx is a component-based Windows application for creating, assessing, and evaluating Bayesian Networks.
- SMILE (Structural Modeling, Inference, and Learning Engine) is a fully portable library of C++ classes implementing graphical decision-theoretic methods, such as Bayesian networks and influence diagrams.
- **UnBBayes:** Framework and GUI for Bayes Nets and other probabilistic models.

Available at: http://teklis.com/10-free-and-open-source-bayesian-network-software/

CHAPTER SUMMARY

In this chapter the influence diagram has been validated using the Monte-Carlo analysis in which each variable takes values from the distribution emerged from the elicitation, instead of using average values as in the influence diagram. Two different scenarios were tested. In the first scenario, initial variables and decisions were set to values obtained by solving the influence diagram. Then the Monte-Carlo simulation with 10 000 trials was ran. Each trial used different values of the variables from the elicited distribution. As the third step, results of both methods were compared and confirmed the matching between them.

The interesting part of the Monte-Carlo simulations was solving the model using an optimization tool available as part of Oracle Crystal Ball. In an attempt to find the optimal solution that maximizes the average value of the utility function, an analysis with 10 000 "what if" scenarios was made and each scenario has changed 10 000 different values of the variables. The value of that simulation is that it takes into account the stochastic nature of the causes of the unavailability of information systems. The optimization result is partially different from the result obtained by solving the influence diagrams, in the sense that this simulation recommends investment in IS monitoring and control, which was not recommended by solving the influence diagram. This difference can be explained by the stochastic character of this model, as opposed to the deterministic nature of the influence diagram. In addition, I used a Monte-Carlo simulation to make the analysis of optimal levels of investment for achieving IS availability levels between 99% to 99.9% in steps of 0.01%. The results I got running this simulation correspond to the results obtained using the influence diagram.

REFERENCES

Franke, U., Johnson, P., König, J., & von Würtemberg, L. M. (2012). Availability of enterprise IT systems: An expert-based Bayesian framework. *Software Quality Journal, 20*(2), 369–394. doi:10.1007/s11219-011-9141-z

Ibrahimovic, S., & Bajgoric, N. (2016). Modeling Information System Availability by Using Bayesian Belief Network Approach. *Interdisciplinary Description of Complex Systems, 14*(2), 125–138. doi:10.7906/indecs.14.2.2

Kahneman, D., & Tversky, A. (1979). Prospect theory: An analysis of decision under risk. *Econometrica, 47*(2), 263–291. doi:10.2307/1914185

Marcus, E., & Stern, H. (2003). *Blueprints for high availability*. John Wiley & Sons.

Neil, M., & Fenton, N. (2008). Using Bayesian networks to model the operational risk to information technology infrastructure in financial institutions. *Journal of Financial Transformation, 22*, 131–138.

Conclusion

In today's world, most of the business activities are associated with the use of information technology (IT). Information technologies enable and facilitate business, while, at the same time, business success is becoming increasingly dependent on the adequate use of information technologies and on risks associated with this dependence. The availability of information system (IS) is an essential requirement that business presents to IT departments. According to ITIL, availability is the characteristic of the IS to perform its agreed action at the request of an authorized user (Taylor et al., 2007). Availability in the broader sense implies that the information system is ready to serve end users, even in the event of unforeseen and catastrophic events, and that, at the same time, it is protected from various security threats.

From the availability perspective, in this study, the system was regarded as a set of services that are available to end users. The total availability of an information system is the result of summarizing the availability of individual services as a system components. It is assumed that each service has an agreed-upon operation time (if service is to be continuously available 24x7 or only 8x5). The percentage of users affected by the outage of individual systems is also considered.

This book contains an exhaustive review of the literature on the IS availability field, looking at this issue from various perspectives. Primarily, the book presents the works of other researchers who dealt with the concept of availability and provide information about the current state of knowledge in the area of models and tools for assessing, measuring and predicting an IS availability. The economic aspect was also addressed with regard to investments in improving the availability of information systems. The main conclusion is that the economic aspect of investing in availability in previous studies was most often viewed through the prism of investment in information security. Particular emphasis in this book was given to a theoretical overview of Bayesian networks and influence diagrams, by providing an overview of the applications of Bayesian networks in the fields of operational risk and information security. In the central part of the book, the optimization model of the investment in IT infrastructure was constructed, with the main objective of improving the availability of information systems. The theoretical framework for the model was von Neumann-Morgenstern's utility theory, and the model was implemented using influence diagrams. Information on systems outages that would be the base for modeling using historical data (provided that an organization keeps failures track and their causes) are not publicly available. Therefore, because BBN can combine statistical and qualitative data, and to map the causal structure of the process (Neil et al., 2008), authors selected it as a modeling tool in this study.

As a starting point for the selection of variables that affect the availability of information system, the research presented by Franke et al. (2012) was used. Their choice of variables was based on "the index of availability" (Marcus & Stern, 2003), adopted by Franke (2014) and Ibrahimovic and Bajgoric (2016). At the end, we presented a model that consists of thirteen variables representing thirteen domains affecting information systems availability. If the best practices are implemented in one more of those domains, IS unavailability could be reduced. The probability elicitation used for determining model parameters was done by interviewing 23 relevant experts with adequate experience in the availability of IT systems. During the elicitation, most experts agreed that the selection of variables in the model is adequate and that the model is comprehensive. Elicitation was conducted through structured interviews. In the first part of interviews, training of experts and the calibration of their predictions was carried out, while in the second part experts filled in the questionnaire. The questionnaire consisted of three sets of questions. Experts were first asked to estimate the impact of individual variables on system availability. In the second question, experts gave their assessment of the situation in the areas described by the variables. To answer the third question, they estimated the necessary investments to bring the field represented by variable to the level of best practices.

Our research has shown that managing availability requirements makes the greatest impact on the availability (23.20%), followed by operations management (20.54%) and the location and equipment of the disaster recovery site (19.52%). The reduction of IS unavailability is least impacted by the physical environment (10.53%), followed by backup management (11.05%) and server platforms (11.81%). Research results showed that the state of implementation of best practices in the areas described by variables ranges from 4.60 to 6.85 on a scale from 1 to 10 depending on the area. According to the results of this research, the perception of experts is that the state of the essential IS infrastructure elements, including the server room, server and network infrastructure, data redundancy, backup management is much better than the process part, which includes change management, operations management, monitoring and requirements management. Assessment of current maturity level of backup management may explain why the experts estimated that implementing best practices in that area would have a small impact on reducing unavailability, as the situation in that field has been assessed as the best compared to all other areas that were part of the model. A similar explanation applies to the physical environment and server infrastructure. The above was the main reason to include assessed states of implementing best practices in the field as the prior probability for each parent node in BBN-based "Leaky Noisy-OR" model. The conditional probability table for the node that represents availability is filled based on a linear transformation of the elicited impact values. The model is set up assuming the initial system availability of 99% and a leak of 0.01%, which represents the unavailability of the system. This occurred under the influence of unmodeled causes. Both of these parameters can be subsequently changed.

The influence diagram, based on the Utility Theory, was developed on top of the BBN model for optimizing IT infrastructure investments. The investment cost, to reach best practice in the particular area, was obtained by expert elicitation. Only IT managers of the banks were asked to estimate the investment required. Responses were weighted by dividing investment amount by the size of organization assets, to be independent of the organization size. The utility function, which was used in the model, was a linear function that represents the total loss due to the unavailability of the system and investments costs necessary to bring variables to the level of best practices. The goal of the model was to maximize the expected utility, with the restrictions imposed by the desired level of availability. When solving the model without limit imposed to the availability level was tried, the optimal level of investment was very low (in this case only investment in requirements management and monitoring). Main reasons for that were relatively high (99%) initial level of IS availability, and diminishing return for investments made to raise availability level above 99.5%. On the other hand, there are regulations with regard to IS management in all national banking sectors which impose the application of best practices in specific areas represented in the model. Another reason for investing could be the risk avoidance attitude adopted by a bank management. Those two reasons could be the driving force for investing above the optimal level.

Comparing the results of this research with the ITIL investment/availability curve, which represents the ratio of availability and investment cost, it can be concluded that the results of research matched the ITIL graph in two aspects, shape of the curve and the fact that the most expensive investments are required in the domains of data redundancy and designing highly available client-server systems. Although the utility function does not have the maximum value if an investment is made to achieve the best practice level in the IS monitoring and control area, one-dimensional tornado analysis has shown that investment in that area should be made. The main reason for investing is that 25% percentage variation in the dependent variable can be eliminated if the best practice level in that field is achieved. The influence diagram was validated using the Monte-Carlo analysis in which each variable took values from the distribution emerged from the elicitation, instead of using average values as in the influence diagram. Two different scenarios were tested. In the first scenario, initial variables and decisions were set to values obtained by solving the influence diagram. Then the Monte-Carlo simulation with 10,000 trials was ran. Every trial used different values of the variables from the elicited distribution. As the third step, results of both methods were compared and confirmed the matching between them.

The interesting part of the Monte-Carlo simulations was solving the model using an optimization tool available as part of Oracle Crystal Ball. In an attempt to find the optimal solution that maximizes the average value of the utility function, an analysis with 10,000 "what if" scenarios were made and in each scenario 10,000 different values of the variables were changed. The value of that simulation is that it takes into account the stochastic nature of the causes of the unavailability of information systems. The optimization result is partially different from the result obtained by solving the influence diagrams, in the sense that this simulation recommends investment in IS monitoring and control, which was not recommended by solving the influence diagram. This difference can be explained by the stochastic character of this model, as opposed to the deterministic nature of the influence diagram. In addition, a Monte-Carlo simulation was used to make the analysis of optimal levels of investment for achieving IS availability levels between 99% to 99.9% in steps of 0.01%.

LIMITATIONS AND RECOMMENDATION FOR A FUTURE RESEARCH

Models are simplified picture of reality, therefore this model too is based on several assumptions. The basic premise built in this model is the independence of variables that was prerequisite for the application of Leaky Noisy-OR BBN. This assumption is based on the fact that each variable may independently, cause the system unavailability. The correlations between the variables are modeled through the power of influence of individual causes on the effect that are integral parts of a conditional probabilities table.

The second limitation is the binary representation of decision variables, because an investment in a domain does not result always in bringing this domain to the best practice level. Instead, investments most often improve the maturity level in the domain, thus reducing the probability that the domain, which was invested in, will cause the system unavailability. That is, the total investment budget for rising availability level can be deployed to remedy the situation in several areas (e.g. five) instead of on achieving best practice in only two. Further studies would be of interests to work on a model that would overcome this limitation by using continuous variables instead of using binary and Noisy-MAX node instead of Noisy-OR.

Additional limitation is linearity of utility function, used in the model, and using function expected monetary value as a utility function. Recent studies in the decision analysis based on "Prospect Theory" (Kahneman & Tversky, 1979), demonstrated that while deciding one does not always behave rationally. People make decisions based on the potential value losses and gains, and not the value of the outcome, and they are using various heuristics and biases in assessment of profits and losses. It would be interesting to construct the utility function using this theory that would reflect the preferences of decision makers toward a risk taking.

The opinions of all experts who participated are treated equally, regardless of age, experience, size of the organization in which they work or the complexity of the system it operates, a number of organizations for which they worked during their careers. The recommendation would be to work further to develop a system for weighting the opinions of experts, considering specified criteria.

In addition to this, in the future research, it is recommended to improve the modeling of unavailability costs. Main area for improvement is, for example, modeling of unavailability threshold which may cause losing clients, or a networking effect initiated by spreading negative information about the quality of service.

As a final recommendation for further research, the authors suggest further empirical validation of the model, based on unavailability of data combined with incident data, gathered from real world cases.

REFERENCES

Franke, U., Johnson, P., König, J., & von Würtemberg, L. M. (2012). Availability of enterprise IT systems: An expert-based Bayesian framework. *Software Quality Journal, 20*(2), 369–394. doi:10.1007/s11219-011-9141-z

Ibrahimovic, S., & Bajgoric, N. (2016). Modeling Information System Availability by Using Bayesian Belief Network Approach. *Interdisciplinary Description of Complex Systems, 14*(2), 125–138. doi:10.7906/indecs.14.2.2

Kahneman, D., & Tversky, A. (1979). Prospect theory: An analysis of decision under risk. *Econometrica, 47*(2), 263–291. doi:10.2307/1914185

Marcus, E., & Stern, H. (2003). *Blueprints for high availability*. John Wiley & Sons.

Neil, M., & Fenton, N. (2008). Using Bayesian networks to model the operational risk to information technology infrastructure in financial institutions. *Journal of Financial Transformation, 22*, 131–138.

Related Readings

To continue IGI Global's long-standing tradition of advancing innovation through emerging research, please find below a compiled list of recommended IGI Global book chapters and journal articles in the areas of data storage, decentralized computing, and the internet of things. These related readings will provide additional information and guidance to further enrich your knowledge and assist you with your own research.

Abidi, N., Bandyopadhayay, A., & Gupta, V. (2017). Sustainable Supply Chain Management: A Three Dimensional Framework and Performance Metric for Indian IT Product Companies. *International Journal of Information Systems and Supply Chain Management*, *10*(1), 29–52. doi:10.4018/IJISSCM.2017010103

Achahbar, O., & Abid, M. R. (2015). The Impact of Virtualization on High Performance Computing Clustering in the Cloud. *International Journal of Distributed Systems and Technologies*, *6*(4), 65–81. doi:10.4018/IJDST.2015100104

Adhikari, M., Das, A., & Mukherjee, A. (2016). Utility Computing and Its Utilization. In G. Deka, G. Siddesh, K. Srinivasa, & L. Patnaik (Eds.), *Emerging Research Surrounding Power Consumption and Performance Issues in Utility Computing* (pp. 1–21). Hershey, PA: IGI Global. doi:10.4018/978-1-4666-8853-7.ch001

Aggarwal, S., & Nayak, A. (2016). Mobile Big Data: A New Frontier of Innovation. In J. Aguado, C. Feijóo, & I. Martínez (Eds.), *Emerging Perspectives on the Mobile Content Evolution* (pp. 138–158). Hershey, PA: IGI Global. doi:10.4018/978-1-4666-8838-4.ch008

Akherfi, K., Harroud, H., & Gerndt, M. (2016). A Mobile Cloud Middleware to Support Mobility and Cloud Interoperability. *International Journal of Adaptive, Resilient and Autonomic Systems*, 7(1), 41–58. doi:10.4018/IJARAS.2016010103

Al-Hamami, M. A. (2015). The Impact of Big Data on Security. In A. Al-Hamami & G. Waleed al-Saadoon (Eds.), *Handbook of Research on Threat Detection and Countermeasures in Network Security* (pp. 276–298). Hershey, PA: IGI Global. doi:10.4018/978-1-4666-6583-5.ch015

Al Jabri, H. A., Al-Badi, A. H., & Ali, O. (2017). Exploring the Usage of Big Data Analytical Tools in Telecommunication Industry in Oman. *Information Resources Management Journal*, 30(1), 1–14. doi:10.4018/IRMJ.2017010101

Alohali, B. (2016). Security in Cloud of Things (CoT). In Z. Ma (Ed.), *Managing Big Data in Cloud Computing Environments* (pp. 46–70). Hershey, PA: IGI Global. doi:10.4018/978-1-4666-9834-5.ch003

Alohali, B. (2017). Detection Protocol of Possible Crime Scenes Using Internet of Things (IoT). In M. Moore (Ed.), *Cybersecurity Breaches and Issues Surrounding Online Threat Protection* (pp. 175–196). Hershey, PA: IGI Global. doi:10.4018/978-1-5225-1941-6.ch008

AlZain, M. A., Li, A. S., Soh, B., & Pardede, E. (2015). Multi-Cloud Data Management using Shamirs Secret Sharing and Quantum Byzantine Agreement Schemes. *International Journal of Cloud Applications and Computing*, 5(3), 35–52. doi:10.4018/IJCAC.2015070103

Armstrong, S., & Yampolskiy, R. V. (2017). Security Solutions for Intelligent and Complex Systems. In M. Dawson, M. Eltayeb, & M. Omar (Eds.), *Security Solutions for Hyperconnectivity and the Internet of Things* (pp. 37–88). Hershey, PA: IGI Global. doi:10.4018/978-1-5225-0741-3.ch003

Attasena, V., Harbi, N., & Darmont, J. (2015). A Novel Multi-Secret Sharing Approach for Secure Data Warehousing and On-Line Analysis Processing in the Cloud. *International Journal of Data Warehousing and Mining*, 11(2), 22–43. doi:10.4018/ijdwm.2015040102

Awad, W. S., & Abdullah, H. M. (2014). Improving the Security of Storage Systems: Bahrain Case Study. *International Journal of Mobile Computing and Multimedia Communications*, 6(3), 75–105. doi:10.4018/IJMCMC.2014070104

Bagui, S., & Nguyen, L. T. (2015). Database Sharding: To Provide Fault Tolerance and Scalability of Big Data on the Cloud. *International Journal of Cloud Applications and Computing, 5*(2), 36–52. doi:10.4018/IJCAC.2015040103

Barbierato, E., Gribaudo, M., & Iacono, M. (2016). Modeling and Evaluating the Effects of Big Data Storage Resource Allocation in Global Scale Cloud Architectures. *International Journal of Data Warehousing and Mining, 12*(2), 1–20. doi:10.4018/IJDWM.2016040101

Barbosa, J. L., Barbosa, D. N., Rigo, S. J., Machado de Oliveira, J., & Junior, S. A. (2017). Collaborative Learning on Decentralized Ubiquitous Environments. In L. Tomei (Ed.), *Exploring the New Era of Technology-Infused Education* (pp. 141–157). Hershey, PA: IGI Global. doi:10.4018/978-1-5225-1709-2.ch009

Benmounah, Z., Meshoul, S., & Batouche, M. (2017). Scalable Differential Evolutionary Clustering Algorithm for Big Data Using Map-Reduce Paradigm. *International Journal of Applied Metaheuristic Computing, 8*(1), 45–60. doi:10.4018/IJAMC.2017010103

Bhadoria, R. S. (2016). Performance of Enterprise Architecture in Utility Computing. In G. Deka, G. Siddesh, K. Srinivasa, & L. Patnaik (Eds.), *Emerging Research Surrounding Power Consumption and Performance Issues in Utility Computing* (pp. 44–68). Hershey, PA: IGI Global. doi:10.4018/978-1-4666-8853-7.ch003

Bhardwaj, A. (2017). Solutions for Securing End User Data over the Cloud Deployed Applications. In M. Moore (Ed.), *Cybersecurity Breaches and Issues Surrounding Online Threat Protection* (pp. 198–218). Hershey, PA: IGI Global; doi:10.4018/978-1-5225-1941-6.ch009

Bibi, S., Katsaros, D., & Bozanis, P. (2015). Cloud Computing Economics. In V. Díaz, J. Lovelle, & B. García-Bustelo (Eds.), *Handbook of Research on Innovations in Systems and Software Engineering* (pp. 125–149). Hershey, PA: IGI Global. doi:10.4018/978-1-4666-6359-6.ch005

Bihl, T. J., Young, W. A. II, & Weckman, G. R. (2016). Defining, Understanding, and Addressing Big Data. *International Journal of Business Analytics, 3*(2), 1–32. doi:10.4018/IJBAN.2016040101

Bimonte, S., Sautot, L., Journaux, L., & Faivre, B. (2017). Multidimensional Model Design using Data Mining: A Rapid Prototyping Methodology. *International Journal of Data Warehousing and Mining, 13*(1), 1–35. doi:10.4018/IJDWM.2017010101

Bruno, G. (2017). A Dataflow-Oriented Modeling Approach to Business Processes. *International Journal of Human Capital and Information Technology Professionals, 8*(1), 51–65. doi:10.4018/IJHCITP.2017010104

Chande, S. V. (2014). Cloud Database Systems: NoSQL, NewSQL, and Hybrid. In P. Raj & G. Deka (Eds.), *Handbook of Research on Cloud Infrastructures for Big Data Analytics* (pp. 216–231). Hershey, PA: IGI Global. doi:10.4018/978-1-4666-5864-6.ch009

Copie, A. Manațe, B., Munteanu, V. I., & Fortiș, T. (2015). An Internet of Things Governance Architecture with Applications in Healthcare. In F. Xhafa, P. Moore, & G. Tadros (Eds.), Advanced Technological Solutions for E-Health and Dementia Patient Monitoring (pp. 322-344). Hershey, PA: IGI Global. doi:10.4018/978-1-4666-7481-3.ch013

Cordeschi, N., Shojafar, M., Amendola, D., & Baccarelli, E. (2015). Energy-Saving QoS Resource Management of Virtualized Networked Data Centers for Big Data Stream Computing. In S. Bagchi (Ed.), *Emerging Research in Cloud Distributed Computing Systems* (pp. 122–155). Hershey, PA: IGI Global. doi:10.4018/978-1-4666-8213-9.ch004

Costan, A. A., Iancu, B., Rasa, P. C., Radu, A., Peculea, A., & Dadarlat, V. T. (2017). Intercloud: Delivering Innovative Cloud Services. In I. Hosu & I. Iancu (Eds.), *Digital Entrepreneurship and Global Innovation* (pp. 59–78). Hershey, PA: IGI Global. doi:10.4018/978-1-5225-0953-0.ch004

Croatti, A., Ricci, A., & Viroli, M. (2017). Towards a Mobile Augmented Reality System for Emergency Management: The Case of SAFE. *International Journal of Distributed Systems and Technologies, 8*(1), 46–58. doi:10.4018/IJDST.2017010104

David-West, O. (2016). Information and Communications Technology (ICT) and the Supply Chain. In B. Christiansen (Ed.), *Handbook of Research on Global Supply Chain Management* (pp. 495–515). Hershey, PA: IGI Global. doi:10.4018/978-1-4666-9639-6.ch028

Dawson, M. (2017). Exploring Secure Computing for the Internet of Things, Internet of Everything, Web of Things, and Hyperconnectivity. In M. Dawson, M. Eltayeb, & M. Omar (Eds.), *Security Solutions for Hyperconnectivity and the Internet of Things* (pp. 1–12). Hershey, PA: IGI Global. doi:10.4018/978-1-5225-0741-3.ch001

Delgado, J. C. (2015). An Interoperability Framework for Enterprise Applications in Cloud Environments. In N. Rao (Ed.), *Enterprise Management Strategies in the Era of Cloud Computing* (pp. 26–59). Hershey, PA: IGI Global. doi:10.4018/978-1-4666-8339-6.ch002

Dhal, S. K., Verma, H., & Addya, S. K. (2017). Resource and Energy Efficient Virtual Machine Migration in Cloud Data Centers. In A. Turuk, B. Sahoo, & S. Addya (Eds.), *Resource Management and Efficiency in Cloud Computing Environments* (pp. 210–238). Hershey, PA: IGI Global. doi:10.4018/978-1-5225-1721-4.ch009

Duggirala, S. (2014). Big Data Architecture: Storage and Computation. In P. Raj & G. Deka (Eds.), *Handbook of Research on Cloud Infrastructures for Big Data Analytics* (pp. 129–156). Hershey, PA: IGI Global. doi:10.4018/978-1-4666-5864-6.ch006

Easton, J., & Parmar, R. (2017). Navigating Your Way to the Hybrid Cloud. In J. Chen, Y. Zhang, & R. Gottschalk (Eds.), *Handbook of Research on End-to-End Cloud Computing Architecture Design* (pp. 15–38). Hershey, PA: IGI Global. doi:10.4018/978-1-5225-0759-8.ch002

Elkabbany, G. F., & Rasslan, M. (2017). Security Issues in Distributed Computing System Models. In M. Dawson, M. Eltayeb, & M. Omar (Eds.), *Security Solutions for Hyperconnectivity and the Internet of Things* (pp. 211–259). Hershey, PA: IGI Global. doi:10.4018/978-1-5225-0741-3.ch009

Elkhodr, M., Shahrestani, S., & Cheung, H. (2016). Wireless Enabling Technologies for the Internet of Things. In Q. Hassan (Ed.), *Innovative Research and Applications in Next-Generation High Performance Computing* (pp. 368–396). Hershey, PA: IGI Global. doi:10.4018/978-1-5225-0287-6.ch015

Elkhodr, M., Shahrestani, S., & Cheung, H. (2017). Internet of Things Research Challenges. In M. Dawson, M. Eltayeb, & M. Omar (Eds.), *Security Solutions for Hyperconnectivity and the Internet of Things* (pp. 13–36). Hershey, PA: IGI Global. doi:10.4018/978-1-5225-0741-3.ch002

Erturk, E. (2017). Cloud Computing and Cybersecurity Issues Facing Local Enterprises. In M. Moore (Ed.), *Cybersecurity Breaches and Issues Surrounding Online Threat Protection* (pp. 219–247). Hershey, PA: IGI Global. doi:10.4018/978-1-5225-1941-6.ch010

Ferreira da Silva, R., Glatard, T., & Desprez, F. (2015). Self-Management of Operational Issues for Grid Computing: The Case of the Virtual Imaging Platform. In S. Bagchi (Ed.), *Emerging Research in Cloud Distributed Computing Systems* (pp. 187–221). Hershey, PA: IGI Global. doi:10.4018/978-1-4666-8213-9.ch006

Fu, S., He, L., Liao, X., Huang, C., Li, K., & Chang, C. (2015). Analyzing and Boosting the Data Availability in Decentralized Online Social Networks. *International Journal of Web Services Research*, *12*(2), 47–72. doi:10.4018/IJWSR.2015040103

Gao, F., & Zhao, Q. (2014). Big Data Based Logistics Data Mining Platform: Architecture and Implementation. *International Journal of Interdisciplinary Telecommunications and Networking*, *6*(4), 24–34. doi:10.4018/IJITN.2014100103

Gudivada, V. N., Nandigam, J., & Paris, J. (2015). Programming Paradigms in High Performance Computing. In R. Segall, J. Cook, & Q. Zhang (Eds.), *Research and Applications in Global Supercomputing* (pp. 303–330). Hershey, PA: IGI Global. doi:10.4018/978-1-4666-7461-5.ch013

Hagos, D. H. (2016). Software-Defined Networking for Scalable Cloud-based Services to Improve System Performance of Hadoop-based Big Data Applications. *International Journal of Grid and High Performance Computing*, *8*(2), 1–22. doi:10.4018/IJGHPC.2016040101

Hallappanavar, V. L., & Birje, M. N. (2017). Trust Management in Cloud Computing. In M. Dawson, M. Eltayeb, & M. Omar (Eds.), *Security Solutions for Hyperconnectivity and the Internet of Things* (pp. 151–183). Hershey, PA: IGI Global. doi:10.4018/978-1-5225-0741-3.ch007

Hameur Laine, A., & Brahimi, S. (2017). Background on Context-Aware Computing Systems. In C. Reis & M. Maximiano (Eds.), *Internet of Things and Advanced Application in Healthcare* (pp. 1–31). Hershey, PA: IGI Global. doi:10.4018/978-1-5225-1820-4.ch001

Hamidi, H. (2017). A Model for Impact of Organizational Project Benefits Management and its Impact on End User. *Journal of Organizational and End User Computing*, *29*(1), 51–65. doi:10.4018/JOEUC.2017010104

Hamidine, H., & Mahmood, A. (2017). Cloud Computing Data Storage Security Based on Different Encryption Schemes. In J. Chen, Y. Zhang, & R. Gottschalk (Eds.), *Handbook of Research on End-to-End Cloud Computing Architecture Design* (pp. 189–221). Hershey, PA: IGI Global. doi:10.4018/978-1-5225-0759-8.ch009

Hamidine, H., & Mahmood, A. (2017). Cloud Computing Data Storage Security Based on Different Encryption Schemes. In J. Chen, Y. Zhang, & R. Gottschalk (Eds.), *Handbook of Research on End-to-End Cloud Computing Architecture Design* (pp. 189–221). Hershey, PA: IGI Global. doi:10.4018/978-1-5225-0759-8.ch009

Hao, Y., & Helo, P. (2015). Cloud Manufacturing towards Sustainable Management. In F. Soliman (Ed.), *Business Transformation and Sustainability through Cloud System Implementation* (pp. 121–139). Hershey, PA: IGI Global. doi:10.4018/978-1-4666-6445-6.ch009

Hasan, N., & Rahman, A. A. (2017). Ranking the Factors that Impact Customers Online Participation in Value Co-creation in Service Sector Using Analytic Hierarchy Process. *International Journal of Information Systems in the Service Sector*, 9(1), 37–53. doi:10.4018/IJISSS.2017010103

Hashemi, S., Monfaredi, K., & Hashemi, S. Y. (2015). Cloud Computing for Secure Services in E-Government Architecture. *Journal of Information Technology Research*, 8(1), 43–61. doi:10.4018/JITR.2015010104

Hayajneh, S. M. (2015). Cloud Computing SaaS Paradigm for Efficient Modelling of Solar Features and Activities. *International Journal of Cloud Applications and Computing*, 5(3), 20–34. doi:10.4018/IJCAC.2015070102

Huang, L. K. (2017). A Cultural Model of Online Banking Adoption: Long-Term Orientation Perspective. *Journal of Organizational and End User Computing*, 29(1), 1–22. doi:10.4018/JOEUC.2017010101

Jacob, G., & Annamalai, M. (2017). Secure Storage and Transmission of Healthcare Records. In V. Tiwari, B. Tiwari, R. Thakur, & S. Gupta (Eds.), *Pattern and Data Analysis in Healthcare Settings* (pp. 7–34). Hershey, PA: IGI Global. doi:10.4018/978-1-5225-0536-5.ch002

Jadon, K. S., Mudgal, P., & Bhadoria, R. S. (2016). Optimization and Management of Resource in Utility Computing. In G. Deka, G. Siddesh, K. Srinivasa, & L. Patnaik (Eds.), *Emerging Research Surrounding Power Consumption and Performance Issues in Utility Computing* (pp. 22–43). Hershey, PA: IGI Global. doi:10.4018/978-1-4666-8853-7.ch002

Jararweh, Y., Al-Sharqawi, O., Abdulla, N., Tawalbeh, L., & Alhammouri, M. (2014). High-Throughput Encryption for Cloud Computing Storage System. *International Journal of Cloud Applications and Computing, 4*(2), 1–14. doi:10.4018/ijcac.2014040101

Jha, M., Jha, S., & O'Brien, L. (2017). Social Media and Big Data: A Conceptual Foundation for Organizations. In R. Chugh (Ed.), *Harnessing Social Media as a Knowledge Management Tool* (pp. 315–332). Hershey, PA: IGI Global. doi:10.4018/978-1-5225-0495-5.ch015

Kantarci, B., & Mouftah, H. T. (2015). Sensing as a Service in Cloud-Centric Internet of Things Architecture. In T. Soyata (Ed.), *Enabling Real-Time Mobile Cloud Computing through Emerging Technologies* (pp. 83–115). Hershey, PA: IGI Global. doi:10.4018/978-1-4666-8662-5.ch003

Kasemsap, K. (2015). The Role of Cloud Computing Adoption in Global Business. In V. Chang, R. Walters, & G. Wills (Eds.), *Delivery and Adoption of Cloud Computing Services in Contemporary Organizations* (pp. 26–55). Hershey, PA: IGI Global. doi:10.4018/978-1-4666-8210-8.ch002

Kasemsap, K. (2015). The Role of Cloud Computing in Global Supply Chain. In N. Rao (Ed.), *Enterprise Management Strategies in the Era of Cloud Computing* (pp. 192–219). Hershey, PA: IGI Global. doi:10.4018/978-1-4666-8339-6.ch009

Kasemsap, K. (2017). Mastering Intelligent Decision Support Systems in Enterprise Information Management. In G. Sreedhar (Ed.), *Web Data Mining and the Development of Knowledge-Based Decision Support Systems* (pp. 35–56). Hershey, PA: IGI Global. doi:10.4018/978-1-5225-1877-8.ch004

Kaukalias, T., & Chatzimisios, P. (2015). Internet of Things (IoT). In M. Khosrow-Pour (Ed.), *Encyclopedia of Information Science and Technology* (3rd ed., pp. 7623–7632). Hershey, PA: IGI Global. doi:10.4018/978-1-4666-5888-2.ch751

Kavoura, A., & Koziol, L. (2017). Polish Firms' Innovation Capability for Competitiveness via Information Technologies and Social Media Implementation. In A. Vlachvei, O. Notta, K. Karantininis, & N. Tsounis (Eds.), *Factors Affecting Firm Competitiveness and Performance in the Modern Business World* (pp. 191–222). Hershey, PA: IGI Global. doi:10.4018/978-1-5225-0843-4.ch007

Khan, I. U., Hameed, Z., & Khan, S. U. (2017). Understanding Online Banking Adoption in a Developing Country: UTAUT2 with Cultural Moderators. *Journal of Global Information Management*, 25(1), 43–65. doi:10.4018/JGIM.2017010103

Kirci, P. (2017). Ubiquitous and Cloud Computing: Ubiquitous Computing. In A. Turuk, B. Sahoo, & S. Addya (Eds.), *Resource Management and Efficiency in Cloud Computing Environments* (pp. 1–32). Hershey, PA: IGI Global. doi:10.4018/978-1-5225-1721-4.ch001

Kofahi, I., & Alryalat, H. (2017). Enterprise Resource Planning (ERP) Implementation Approaches and the Performance of Procure-to-Pay Business Processes: (Field Study in Companies that Implement Oracle ERP in Jordan). *International Journal of Information Technology Project Management*, 8(1), 55–71. doi:10.4018/IJITPM.2017010104

Koumaras, H., Damaskos, C., Diakoumakos, G., Kourtis, M., Xilouris, G., Gardikis, G., & Siakoulis, T. et al. (2015). Virtualization Evolution: From IT Infrastructure Abstraction of Cloud Computing to Virtualization of Network Functions. In G. Mastorakis, C. Mavromoustakis, & E. Pallis (Eds.), *Resource Management of Mobile Cloud Computing Networks and Environments* (pp. 279–306). Hershey, PA: IGI Global. doi:10.4018/978-1-4666-8225-2.ch010

Kuada, E. (2017). Security and Trust in Cloud Computing. In M. Dawson, M. Eltayeb, & M. Omar (Eds.), *Security Solutions for Hyperconnectivity and the Internet of Things* (pp. 184–210). Hershey, PA: IGI Global. doi:10.4018/978-1-5225-0741-3.ch008

Kumar, D., Sahoo, B., & Mandal, T. (2015). Heuristic Task Consolidation Techniques for Energy Efficient Cloud Computing. In N. Rao (Ed.), *Enterprise Management Strategies in the Era of Cloud Computing* (pp. 238–260). Hershey, PA: IGI Global. doi:10.4018/978-1-4666-8339-6.ch011

Lee, C. K., Cao, Y., & Ng, K. H. (2017). Big Data Analytics for Predictive Maintenance Strategies. In H. Chan, N. Subramanian, & M. Abdulrahman (Eds.), *Supply Chain Management in the Big Data Era* (pp. 50–74). Hershey, PA: IGI Global. doi:10.4018/978-1-5225-0956-1.ch004

Liao, W. (2016). Application of Hadoop in the Document Storage Management System for Telecommunication Enterprise. *International Journal of Interdisciplinary Telecommunications and Networking*, 8(2), 58–68. doi:10.4018/IJITN.2016040106

Liew, C. S., Ang, J. M., Goh, Y. T., Koh, W. K., Tan, S. Y., & Teh, R. Y. (2017). Factors Influencing Consumer Acceptance of Internet of Things Technology. In N. Suki (Ed.), *Handbook of Research on Leveraging Consumer Psychology for Effective Customer Engagement* (pp. 186–201). Hershey, PA: IGI Global. doi:10.4018/978-1-5225-0746-8.ch012

Lytras, M. D., Raghavan, V., & Damiani, E. (2017). Big Data and Data Analytics Research: From Metaphors to Value Space for Collective Wisdom in Human Decision Making and Smart Machines. *International Journal on Semantic Web and Information Systems*, 13(1), 1–10. doi:10.4018/IJSWIS.2017010101

Mabe, L. K., & Oladele, O. I. (2017). Application of Information Communication Technologies for Agricultural Development through Extension Services: A Review. In T. Tossy (Ed.), *Information Technology Integration for Socio-Economic Development* (pp. 52–101). Hershey, PA: IGI Global. doi:10.4018/978-1-5225-0539-6.ch003

Machaka, P., & Nelwamondo, F. (2016). Data Mining Techniques for Distributed Denial of Service Attacks Detection in the Internet of Things: A Research Survey. In O. Isafiade & A. Bagula (Eds.), *Data Mining Trends and Applications in Criminal Science and Investigations* (pp. 275–334). Hershey, PA: IGI Global. doi:10.4018/978-1-5225-0463-4.ch010

Manohari, P. K., & Ray, N. K. (2017). A Comprehensive Study of Security in Cloud Computing. In N. Ray & A. Turuk (Eds.), *Handbook of Research on Advanced Wireless Sensor Network Applications, Protocols, and Architectures* (pp. 386–412). Hershey, PA: IGI Global. doi:10.4018/978-1-5225-0486-3.ch016

Manvi, S. S., & Hegde, N. (2017). Vehicular Cloud Computing Challenges and Security. In S. Bhattacharyya, N. Das, D. Bhattacharjee, & A. Mukherjee (Eds.), *Handbook of Research on Recent Developments in Intelligent Communication Application* (pp. 344–365). Hershey, PA: IGI Global. doi:10.4018/978-1-5225-1785-6.ch013

McKelvey, N., Curran, K., & Subaginy, N. (2015). The Internet of Things. In M. Khosrow-Pour (Ed.), *Encyclopedia of Information Science and Technology* (3rd ed., pp. 5777–5783). Hershey, PA: IGI Global. doi:10.4018/978-1-4666-5888-2.ch570

Meddah, I. H., Belkadi, K., & Boudia, M. A. (2017). Efficient Implementation of Hadoop MapReduce based Business Process Dataflow. *International Journal of Decision Support System Technology*, *9*(1), 49–60. doi:10.4018/IJDSST.2017010104

Meghanathan, N. (2015). Virtualization as the Catalyst for Cloud Computing. In M. Khosrow-Pour (Ed.), *Encyclopedia of Information Science and Technology* (3rd ed., pp. 1096–1110). Hershey, PA: IGI Global. doi:10.4018/978-1-4666-5888-2.ch105

Mehenni, T. (2017). Geographic Knowledge Discovery in Multiple Spatial Databases. In S. Faiz & K. Mahmoudi (Eds.), *Handbook of Research on Geographic Information Systems Applications and Advancements* (pp. 344–366). Hershey, PA: IGI Global. doi:10.4018/978-1-5225-0937-0.ch013

Mehrotra, S., & Kohli, S. (2017). Data Clustering and Various Clustering Approaches. In S. Bhattacharyya, S. De, I. Pan, & P. Dutta (Eds.), *Intelligent Multidimensional Data Clustering and Analysis* (pp. 90–108). Hershey, PA: IGI Global. doi:10.4018/978-1-5225-1776-4.ch004

Meralto, C., Moura, J., & Marinheiro, R. (2017). Wireless Mesh Sensor Networks with Mobile Devices: A Comprehensive Review. In N. Ray & A. Turuk (Eds.), *Handbook of Research on Advanced Wireless Sensor Network Applications, Protocols, and Architectures* (pp. 129–155). Hershey, PA: IGI Global. doi:10.4018/978-1-5225-0486-3.ch005

Moradbeikie, A., Abrishami, S., & Abbasi, H. (2016). Creating Time-Limited Attributes for Time-Limited Services in Cloud Computing. *International Journal of Information Security and Privacy*, *10*(4), 44–57. doi:10.4018/IJISP.2016100103

Mourtzoukos, K., Kefalakis, N., & Soldatos, J. (2015). Open Source Object Directory Services for Inter-Enterprise Tracking and Tracing Applications. In I. Lee (Ed.), *RFID Technology Integration for Business Performance Improvement* (pp. 80–97). Hershey, PA: IGI Global. doi:10.4018/978-1-4666-6308-4.ch004

Mugisha, E., Zhang, G., El Abidine, M. Z., & Eugene, M. (2017). A TPM-based Secure Multi-Cloud Storage Architecture grounded on Erasure Codes. *International Journal of Information Security and Privacy*, *11*(1), 52–64. doi:10.4018/IJISP.2017010104

Munir, K. (2017). Security Model for Mobile Cloud Database as a Service (DBaaS). In K. Munir (Ed.), *Security Management in Mobile Cloud Computing* (pp. 169–180). Hershey, PA: IGI Global. doi:10.4018/978-1-5225-0602-7.ch008

Murugaiyan, S. R., Chandramohan, D., Vengattaraman, T., & Dhavachelvan, P. (2014). A Generic Privacy Breach Preventing Methodology for Cloud Based Web Service. *International Journal of Grid and High Performance Computing*, *6*(3), 53–84. doi:10.4018/ijghpc.2014070104

Naeem, M. A., & Jamil, N. (2015). Online Processing of End-User Data in Real-Time Data Warehousing. In M. Usman (Ed.), *Improving Knowledge Discovery through the Integration of Data Mining Techniques* (pp. 13–31). Hershey, PA: IGI Global. doi:10.4018/978-1-4666-8513-0.ch002

Nayak, P. (2017). Internet of Things Services, Applications, Issues, and Challenges. In N. Ray & A. Turuk (Eds.), *Handbook of Research on Advanced Wireless Sensor Network Applications, Protocols, and Architectures* (pp. 353–368). Hershey, PA: IGI Global. doi:10.4018/978-1-5225-0486-3.ch014

Nekaj, E. L. (2017). The Crowd Economy: From the Crowd to Businesses to Public Administrations and Multinational Companies. In W. Vassallo (Ed.), *Crowdfunding for Sustainable Entrepreneurship and Innovation* (pp. 1–19). Hershey, PA: IGI Global. doi:10.4018/978-1-5225-0568-6.ch001

Omar, M. (2015). Cloud Computing Security: Abuse and Nefarious Use of Cloud Computing. In K. Munir, M. Al-Mutairi, & L. Mohammed (Eds.), *Handbook of Research on Security Considerations in Cloud Computing* (pp. 30–38). Hershey, PA: IGI Global; doi:10.4018/978-1-4666-8387-7.ch002

Orike, S., & Brown, D. (2016). Big Data Management: An Investigation into Wireless and Cloud Computing. *International Journal of Interdisciplinary Telecommunications and Networking*, 8(4), 34–50. doi:10.4018/IJITN.2016100104

Ouf, S., & Nasr, M. (2015). Cloud Computing: The Future of Big Data Management. *International Journal of Cloud Applications and Computing*, 5(2), 53–61. doi:10.4018/IJCAC.2015040104

Ozpinar, A., & Yarkan, S. (2016). Vehicle to Cloud: Big Data for Environmental Sustainability, Energy, and Traffic Management. In M. Singh, & D. G. (Eds.), Effective Big Data Management and Opportunities for Implementation (pp. 182-201). Hershey, PA: IGI Global. doi:10.4018/978-1-5225-0182-4.ch012

Pal, A., & Kumar, M. (2017). Collaborative Filtering Based Data Mining for Large Data. In V. Bhatnagar (Ed.), *Collaborative Filtering Using Data Mining and Analysis* (pp. 115–127). Hershey, PA: IGI Global. doi:10.4018/978-1-5225-0489-4.ch006

Pal, K., & Karakostas, B. (2016). A Game-Based Approach for Simulation and Design of Supply Chains. In T. Kramberger, V. Potočan, & V. Ipavec (Eds.), *Sustainable Logistics and Strategic Transportation Planning* (pp. 1–23). Hershey, PA: IGI Global; doi:10.4018/978-1-5225-0001-8.ch001

Panda, S. (2017). Security Issues and Challenges in Internet of Things. In N. Ray & A. Turuk (Eds.), *Handbook of Research on Advanced Wireless Sensor Network Applications, Protocols, and Architectures* (pp. 369–385). Hershey, PA: IGI Global. doi:10.4018/978-1-5225-0486-3.ch015

Pandit, S., Milman, I., Oberhofer, M., & Zhou, Y. (2017). Principled Reference Data Management for Big Data and Business Intelligence. *International Journal of Organizational and Collective Intelligence*, 7(1), 47–66. doi:10.4018/IJOCI.2017010104

Paul, A. K., & Sahoo, B. (2017). Dynamic Virtual Machine Placement in Cloud Computing. In A. Turuk, B. Sahoo, & S. Addya (Eds.), *Resource Management and Efficiency in Cloud Computing Environments* (pp. 136–167). Hershey, PA: IGI Global. doi:10.4018/978-1-5225-1721-4.ch006

Petri, I., Diaz-Montes, J., Zou, M., Zamani, A. R., Beach, T. H., Rana, O. F., & Rezgui, Y. et al. (2016). Distributed Multi-Cloud Based Building Data Analytics. In G. Kecskemeti, A. Kertesz, & Z. Nemeth (Eds.), *Developing Interoperable and Federated Cloud Architecture* (pp. 143–169). Hershey, PA: IGI Global. doi:10.4018/978-1-5225-0153-4.ch006

Poleto, T., Heuer de Carvalho, V. D., & Costa, A. P. (2017). The Full Knowledge of Big Data in the Integration of Inter-Organizational Information: An Approach Focused on Decision Making. *International Journal of Decision Support System Technology*, *9*(1), 16–31. doi:10.4018/IJDSST.2017010102

Rahman, N., & Iverson, S. (2015). Big Data Business Intelligence in Bank Risk Analysis. *International Journal of Business Intelligence Research*, *6*(2), 55–77. doi:10.4018/IJBIR.2015070104

Raj, P. (2014). Big Data Analytics Demystified. In P. Raj & G. Deka (Eds.), *Handbook of Research on Cloud Infrastructures for Big Data Analytics* (pp. 38–73). Hershey, PA: IGI Global. doi:10.4018/978-1-4666-5864-6.ch003

Raj, P. (2014). The Compute Infrastructures for Big Data Analytics. In P. Raj & G. Deka (Eds.), *Handbook of Research on Cloud Infrastructures for Big Data Analytics* (pp. 74–109). Hershey, PA: IGI Global. doi:10.4018/978-1-4666-5864-6.ch004

Raj, P. (2014). The Network Infrastructures for Big Data Analytics. In P. Raj & G. Deka (Eds.), *Handbook of Research on Cloud Infrastructures for Big Data Analytics* (pp. 157–185). Hershey, PA: IGI Global. doi:10.4018/978-1-4666-5864-6.ch007

Raman, A. C. (2014). Storage Infrastructure for Big Data and Cloud. In P. Raj & G. Deka (Eds.), *Handbook of Research on Cloud Infrastructures for Big Data Analytics* (pp. 110–128). Hershey, PA: IGI Global. doi:10.4018/978-1-4666-5864-6.ch005

Rao, A. P. (2017). Discovering Knowledge Hidden in Big Data from Machine-Learning Techniques. In G. Sreedhar (Ed.), *Web Data Mining and the Development of Knowledge-Based Decision Support Systems* (pp. 167–183). Hershey, PA: IGI Global. doi:10.4018/978-1-5225-1877-8.ch010

Rathore, M. M., Paul, A., Ahmad, A., & Jeon, G. (2017). IoT-Based Big Data: From Smart City towards Next Generation Super City Planning. *International Journal on Semantic Web and Information Systems*, *13*(1), 28–47. doi:10.4018/IJSWIS.2017010103

Ratten, V. (2015). An Entrepreneurial Approach to Cloud Computing Design and Application: Technological Innovation and Information System Usage. In S. Aljawarneh (Ed.), *Advanced Research on Cloud Computing Design and Applications* (pp. 1–14). Hershey, PA: IGI Global. doi:10.4018/978-1-4666-8676-2.ch001

Rebekah, R. D., Cheelu, D., & Babu, M. R. (2017). Necessity of Key Aggregation Cryptosystem for Data Sharing in Cloud Computing. In P. Krishna (Ed.), *Emerging Technologies and Applications for Cloud-Based Gaming* (pp. 210–227). Hershey, PA: IGI Global. doi:10.4018/978-1-5225-0546-4.ch010

Rehman, A., Ullah, R., & Abdullah, F. (2015). Big Data Analysis in IoT. In N. Zaman, M. Seliaman, M. Hassan, & F. Marquez (Eds.), *Handbook of Research on Trends and Future Directions in Big Data and Web Intelligence* (pp. 313–327). Hershey, PA: IGI Global. doi:10.4018/978-1-4666-8505-5.ch015

Rehman, M. H., Khan, A. U., & Batool, A. (2016). Big Data Analytics in Mobile and Cloud Computing Environments. In Q. Hassan (Ed.), *Innovative Research and Applications in Next-Generation High Performance Computing* (pp. 349–367). Hershey, PA: IGI Global. doi:10.4018/978-1-5225-0287-6.ch014

Rosado da Cruz, A. M., & Paiva, S. (2016). Cloud and Mobile: A Future Together. In A. Rosado da Cruz & S. Paiva (Eds.), *Modern Software Engineering Methodologies for Mobile and Cloud Environments* (pp. 1–20). Hershey, PA: IGI Global; doi:10.4018/978-1-4666-9916-8.ch001

Rusko, R. (2017). Strategic Turning Points in ICT Business: The Business Development, Transformation, and Evolution in the Case of Nokia. In I. Oncioiu (Ed.), *Driving Innovation and Business Success in the Digital Economy* (pp. 1–15). Hershey, PA: IGI Global. doi:10.4018/978-1-5225-1779-5.ch001

Sahlin, J. P. (2015). Federal Government Application of the Cloud Computing Application Integration Model. In M. Khosrow-Pour (Ed.), *Encyclopedia of Information Science and Technology* (3rd ed., pp. 2735–2744). Hershey, PA: IGI Global. doi:10.4018/978-1-4666-5888-2.ch267

Sahoo, S., Sahoo, B., Turuk, A. K., & Mishra, S. K. (2017). Real Time Task Execution in Cloud Using MapReduce Framework. In A. Turuk, B. Sahoo, & S. Addya (Eds.), *Resource Management and Efficiency in Cloud Computing Environments* (pp. 190–209). Hershey, PA: IGI Global. doi:10.4018/978-1-5225-1721-4.ch008

Schnjakin, M., & Meinel, C. (2014). Solving Security and Availability Challenges in Public Clouds. In A. Kayem & C. Meinel (Eds.), *Information Security in Diverse Computing Environments* (pp. 280–302). Hershey, PA: IGI Global. doi:10.4018/978-1-4666-6158-5.ch015

Shaikh, F. (2017). The Benefits of New Online (Digital) Technologies on Business: Understanding the Impact of Digital on Different Aspects of the Business. In I. Hosu & I. Iancu (Eds.), *Digital Entrepreneurship and Global Innovation* (pp. 1–17). Hershey, PA: IGI Global. doi:10.4018/978-1-5225-0953-0.ch001

Shalan, M. (2017). Cloud Service Footprint (CSF): Utilizing Risk and Governance Directions to Characterize a Cloud Service. In A. Turuk, B. Sahoo, & S. Addya (Eds.), *Resource Management and Efficiency in Cloud Computing Environments* (pp. 61–88). Hershey, PA: IGI Global. doi:10.4018/978-1-5225-1721-4.ch003

Sharma, A., & Tandekar, P. (2017). Cyber Security and Business Growth. In Rajagopal, & R. Behl (Eds.), *Business Analytics and Cyber Security Management in Organizations* (pp. 14-27). Hershey, PA: IGI Global. doi:10.4018/978-1-5225-0902-8.ch002

Shen, Y., Li, Y., Wu, L., Liu, S., & Wen, Q. (2014). Big Data Techniques, Tools, and Applications. In Y. Shen, Y. Li, L. Wu, S. Liu, & Q. Wen (Eds.), *Enabling the New Era of Cloud Computing: Data Security, Transfer, and Management* (pp. 185–212). Hershey, PA: IGI Global. doi:10.4018/978-1-4666-4801-2.ch009

Shen, Y., Li, Y., Wu, L., Liu, S., & Wen, Q. (2014). Cloud Infrastructure: Virtualization. In Y. Shen, Y. Li, L. Wu, S. Liu, & Q. Wen (Eds.), *Enabling the New Era of Cloud Computing: Data Security, Transfer, and Management* (pp. 51–76). Hershey, PA: IGI Global. doi:10.4018/978-1-4666-4801-2.ch003

Siddesh, G. M., Srinivasa, K. G., & Tejaswini, L. (2015). Recent Trends in Cloud Computing Security Issues and Their Mitigation. In G. Deka & S. Bakshi (Eds.), *Handbook of Research on Securing Cloud-Based Databases with Biometric Applications* (pp. 16–46). Hershey, PA: IGI Global. doi:10.4018/978-1-4666-6559-0.ch002

Singh, B., & K.S., J. (2017). Security Management in Mobile Cloud Computing: Security and Privacy Issues and Solutions in Mobile Cloud Computing. In K. Munir (Ed.), *Security Management in Mobile Cloud Computing* (pp. 148-168). Hershey, PA: IGI Global. doi:10.4018/978-1-5225-0602-7.ch007

Singh, J., Gimekar, A. M., & Venkatesan, S. (2017). An Overview of Big Data Security with Hadoop Framework. In M. Kumar (Ed.), *Applied Big Data Analytics in Operations Management* (pp. 165–181). Hershey, PA: IGI Global. doi:10.4018/978-1-5225-0886-1.ch008

Singh, S., & Singh, J. (2017). Management of SME's Semi Structured Data Using Semantic Technique. In M. Kumar (Ed.), *Applied Big Data Analytics in Operations Management* (pp. 133–164). Hershey, PA: IGI Global. doi:10.4018/978-1-5225-0886-1.ch007

Sokolowski, L., & Oussena, S. (2016). Using Big Data in Collaborative Learning. In M. Atzmueller, S. Oussena, & T. Roth-Berghofer (Eds.), *Enterprise Big Data Engineering, Analytics, and Management* (pp. 221–237). Hershey, PA: IGI Global. doi:10.4018/978-1-5225-0293-7.ch013

Soliman, F. (2015). Evaluation of Cloud System Success Factors in Supply-Demand Chains. In F. Soliman (Ed.), *Business Transformation and Sustainability through Cloud System Implementation* (pp. 90–104). Hershey, PA: IGI Global. doi:10.4018/978-1-4666-6445-6.ch007

Srinivasan, S. (2014). Meeting Compliance Requirements while using Cloud Services. In S. Srinivasan (Ed.), *Security, Trust, and Regulatory Aspects of Cloud Computing in Business Environments* (pp. 127–144). Hershey, PA: IGI Global. doi:10.4018/978-1-4666-5788-5.ch007

Sun, X., & Wei, Z. (2015). The Dynamic Data Privacy Protection Strategy Based on the CAP Theory. *International Journal of Interdisciplinary Telecommunications and Networking*, 7(1), 44–56. doi:10.4018/ijitn.2015010104

Sundararajan, S., Bhasi, M., & Pramod, K. (2017). Managing Software Risks in Maintenance Projects, from a Vendor Perspective: A Case Study in Global Software Development. *International Journal of Information Technology Project Management*, 8(1), 35–54. doi:10.4018/IJITPM.2017010103

Sundaresan, M., & Boopathy, D. (2014). Different Perspectives of Cloud Security. In S. Srinivasan (Ed.), *Security, Trust, and Regulatory Aspects of Cloud Computing in Business Environments* (pp. 73–90). Hershey, PA: IGI Global. doi:10.4018/978-1-4666-5788-5.ch004

Sutagundar, A. V., & Hatti, D. (2017). Data Management in Internet of Things. In N. Kamila (Ed.), *Handbook of Research on Wireless Sensor Network Trends, Technologies, and Applications* (pp. 80–97). Hershey, PA: IGI Global. doi:10.4018/978-1-5225-0501-3.ch004

Swacha, J. (2014). Measuring and Managing the Economics of Information Storage. In T. Tsiakis, T. Kargidis, & P. Katsaros (Eds.), *Approaches and Processes for Managing the Economics of Information Systems* (pp. 47–65). Hershey, PA: IGI Global. doi:10.4018/978-1-4666-4983-5.ch003

Swarnkar, M., & Bhadoria, R. S. (2016). Security Aspects in Utility Computing. In G. Deka, G. Siddesh, K. Srinivasa, & L. Patnaik (Eds.), *Emerging Research Surrounding Power Consumption and Performance Issues in Utility Computing* (pp. 262–275). Hershey, PA: IGI Global. doi:10.4018/978-1-4666-8853-7.ch012

Talamantes-Padilla, C. A., García-Alcaráz, J. L., Maldonado-Macías, A. A., Alor-Hernández, G., Sánchéz-Ramírez, C., & Hernández-Arellano, J. L. (2017). Information and Communication Technology Impact on Supply Chain Integration, Flexibility, and Performance. In M. Tavana, K. Szabat, & K. Puranam (Eds.), *Organizational Productivity and Performance Measurements Using Predictive Modeling and Analytics* (pp. 213–234). Hershey, PA: IGI Global. doi:10.4018/978-1-5225-0654-6.ch011

Tang, Z., & Pan, Y. (2015). Big Data Security Management. In N. Zaman, M. Seliaman, M. Hassan, & F. Marquez (Eds.), *Handbook of Research on Trends and Future Directions in Big Data and Web Intelligence* (pp. 53–66). Hershey, PA: IGI Global. doi:10.4018/978-1-4666-8505-5.ch003

Thakur, P. K., & Verma, A. (2015). Process Batch Offloading Method for Mobile-Cloud Computing Platform. *Journal of Cases on Information Technology*, *17*(3), 1–13. doi:10.4018/JCIT.2015070101

Thota, C., Manogaran, G., Lopez, D., & Vijayakumar, V. (2017). Big Data Security Framework for Distributed Cloud Data Centers. In M. Moore (Ed.), *Cybersecurity Breaches and Issues Surrounding Online Threat Protection* (pp. 288–310). Hershey, PA: IGI Global. doi:10.4018/978-1-5225-1941-6.ch012

Toor, G. S., & Ma, M. (2017). Security Issues of Communication Networks in Smart Grid. In M. Ferrag & A. Ahmim (Eds.), *Security Solutions and Applied Cryptography in Smart Grid Communications* (pp. 29–49). Hershey, PA: IGI Global. doi:10.4018/978-1-5225-1829-7.ch002

Wahi, A. K., Medury, Y., & Misra, R. K. (2015). Big Data: Enabler or Challenge for Enterprise 2.0. *International Journal of Service Science, Management, Engineering, and Technology*, *6*(2), 1–17. doi:10.4018/ijssmet.2015040101

Wang, H., Liu, W., & Soyata, T. (2014). Accessing Big Data in the Cloud Using Mobile Devices. In P. Raj & G. Deka (Eds.), *Handbook of Research on Cloud Infrastructures for Big Data Analytics* (pp. 444–470). Hershey, PA: IGI Global. doi:10.4018/978-1-4666-5864-6.ch018

Wang, M., & Kerr, D. (2017). Confidential Data Storage Systems for Wearable Platforms. In A. Marrington, D. Kerr, & J. Gammack (Eds.), *Managing Security Issues and the Hidden Dangers of Wearable Technologies* (pp. 74–97). Hershey, PA: IGI Global. doi:10.4018/978-1-5225-1016-1.ch004

Winter, J. S. (2015). Privacy Challenges for the Internet of Things. In M. Khosrow-Pour (Ed.), *Encyclopedia of Information Science and Technology* (3rd ed., pp. 4373–4383). Hershey, PA: IGI Global. doi:10.4018/978-1-4666-5888-2.ch429

Wolfe, M. (2017). Establishing Governance for Hybrid Cloud and the Internet of Things. In J. Chen, Y. Zhang, & R. Gottschalk (Eds.), *Handbook of Research on End-to-End Cloud Computing Architecture Design* (pp. 300–325). Hershey, PA: IGI Global. doi:10.4018/978-1-5225-0759-8.ch013

Yan, Z. (2014). Trust Management in Mobile Cloud Computing. In *Trust Management in Mobile Environments: Autonomic and Usable Models* (pp. 54–93). Hershey, PA: IGI Global. doi:10.4018/978-1-4666-4765-7.ch004

Zardari, M. A., & Jung, L. T. (2016). Classification of File Data Based on Confidentiality in Cloud Computing using K-NN Classifier. *International Journal of Business Analytics*, *3*(2), 61–78. doi:10.4018/IJBAN.2016040104

Zhang, C., Simon, J. C., & Lee, E. (2016). An Empirical Investigation of Decision Making in IT-Related Dilemmas: Impact of Positive and Negative Consequence Information. *Journal of Organizational and End User Computing*, *28*(4), 73–90. doi:10.4018/JOEUC.2016100105

Zou, J., Wang, Y., & Orgun, M. A. (2015). Modeling Accountable Cloud Services Based on Dynamic Logic for Accountability. *International Journal of Web Services Research*, *12*(3), 48–77. doi:10.4018/IJWSR.2015070103

Index

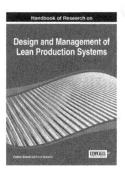
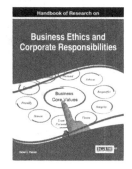

Become an IRMA Member

Members of the **Information Resources Management Association (IRMA)** understand the importance of community within their field of study. The Information Resources Management Association is an ideal venue through which professionals, students, and academicians can convene and share the latest industry innovations and scholarly research that is changing the field of information science and technology. Become a member today and enjoy the benefits of membership as well as the opportunity to collaborate and network with fellow experts in the field.

IRMA Membership Benefits:

- **One FREE Journal Subscription**
- **30% Off Additional Journal Subscriptions**
- **20% Off Book Purchases**
- Updates on the latest events and research on Information Resources Management through the IRMA-L listserv.
- Updates on new open access and downloadable content added to Research IRM.
- A copy of the Information Technology Management Newsletter twice a year.
- A certificate of membership.

IRMA Membership $195

Scan code or visit **irma-international.org** and begin by selecting your free journal subscription.

Membership is good for one full year.

Encyclopedia of Information Science and Technology, Third Edition (10 Vols.)

Mehdi Khosrow-Pour, D.B.A. (Information Resources Management Association, USA)
ISBN: 978-1-4666-5888-2; **EISBN:** 978-1-4666-5889-9; © 2015; 10,384 pages.

The **Encyclopedia of Information Science and Technology, Third Edition** is a 10-volume compilation of authoritative, previously unpublished research-based articles contributed by thousands of researchers and experts from all over the world. This discipline-defining encyclopedia will serve research needs in numerous fields that are affected by the rapid pace and substantial impact of technological change. With an emphasis on modern issues and the presentation of potential opportunities, prospective solutions, and future directions in the field, it is a relevant and essential addition to any academic library's reference collection.

Take An Extra

30% Off [1]

[1] 30% discount offer cannot be combined with any other discount and is only valid on purchases made directly through IGI Global's Online Bookstore (www.igi-global.com/books), not intended for use by distributors or wholesalers. Offer expires December 31, 2016.

Free Lifetime E-Access with Print Purchase

Take 30% Off Retail Price:

Hardcover with Free E-Access:[2] **$2,765**
List Price: $3,950

E-Access with Free Hardcover:[2] **$2,765**
List Price: $3,950

E-Subscription Price:

One (1) Year E-Subscription: $1,288
List Price: $1,840

Two (2) Year E-Subscription: $2,177
List Price: $3,110

Recommend this Title to Your Institution's Library: www.igi-global.com/books

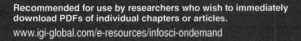